D1447587

A NEW BOOK OF EPITAPHS

By the same author

The History of St Mark's Church, Dewsbury
A Book of Epitaphs
Doncaster Rural District: A Guide
Clarinda: The intimate story of Robert Burns
and Agnes Maclehose
A Book of Superstitions
A Book of Proverbs
Sir Walter Scott's Letters on Demonology & Witchcraft
Robert Burns's Commonplace Book 1783-85
A Book of Witchcraft
Charles Kirkpatrick Sharpe's History of Witchcraft in Scotland
General Trade in Berwick-upon-Tweed 1894
Phantoms, Legends, Customs and Superstitions of the Sea
Robert Burns's Tour of the Borders

A New Book of Epitaphs

By

RAYMOND LAMONT BROWN

FRANK GRAHAM
6 Queen's Terrace, Newcastle upon Tyne, 2

SBN 902833 58 8

Composed in 11-pt Pilgrim and printed in Great Britain by
Northumberland Press Limited
Gateshead

DEDICATION

to

my doughty ancestor
Baron de Bohan du Château de la Mont
(1021–1115)
whose
epitaph was
Dextérité et Agilité
which signified
his dexterity in fiddling the monastic
accounts and agility in scaling the
nunnery wall

CONTENTS

INTRODUCTION

By The Most Rev. His Grace the Lord Archbishop of York

I am glad that Mr Lamont Brown has produced *A New Book of Epitaphs*. Clearly he has spent much time and care in gathering his collection from widely scattered sources.

Here, obviously, is a book which asks to be read, not straight through, but in small doses. There is food for thought here—

> Her Life approach'd so near to Life divine
> That she appear'd while this rough Earth she trod
> A spotless Temple of the living God—

what greater ambition could a man or woman have than to approximate such a character description?

There is rough and ready humour here, sometimes a flippancy in regard to death which contrasts with the seriousness with which the Biblical writers invariably deal with the subject. Does this flippancy cover a fear on the part of the writers in face of a fact with which all humans have to come to terms? Perhaps it is to be regretted that all too few epitaphs reflect the quiet confidence of a St Paul who, looking death in the face, found it desirable, for it meant to him 'to be with Christ', and thus was 'far better'.

Hidden in the lofts and cupboards of many homes there are old family records and letters which cast much needed light on facets of English life and history which can all too readily be lost and forgotten. As I looked through this *New Book of Epitaphs* it occurred to me that the collector, in presenting and annotating these epitaphs, had rescued from oblivion much local information, lore, and humour which otherwise would have been lost to us. I for one am grateful.

Bishopthorpe, Donald Ebor:
York.

AUTHOR'S PREFACE

My first volume of epitaphs *A Book of Epitaphs* (David & Charles/Taplinger Inc 1967 & 1969) was completed in the sincere belief that graveyard inscriptions could add much to current knowledge of social and local history. No less that they included, often in rustic terms, early attempts at pastoral doggerel, fable and folklore and represented some of the best spontaneous and unconscious humour which would have otherwise been lost to succeeding generations.

At the time of publication I had no idea that the book would become a 'best seller' necessitating reprints, and that the text would draw favourable letters from all over the world.

It is my pleasure, therefore, to publicly and collectively thank all those who have written to me from America, New Zealand, Japan, Sweden, Germany and Fiji communicating their enjoyment of the book's content. I would further like to thank the scores of British and American people who have sent me epitaph notes, cuttings and drawings for my collection. Furthermore I would like to express my gratitude to the BBC, ITV and American broadcasting networks for their interest and publicity.

Tweedmouth, Berwick-upon-Tweed RAYMOND LAMONT BROWN
Northumberland, England
January 1973

They Chose Unhallowed Ground

'It seemed the most God-forsaken country in the world ... One fellow said he knew this was the Creator's dumping ground where he had left the worthless dregs after making a world, and the devil had scraped these together a little ...'

That is how William Manly described Death Valley in 1849. Even though Death Valley is now a National Monument stretching in a wide one hundred and forty mile long belt from Saratoga Spring, California, to Bullfrog Hills, Nevada, its mountain ranges and deep canyons are no more hospitable with the passing of more than a hundred years.

Only one reason could have brought men and women anywhere near the 3000 square miles of Death Valley—gold—and the price they had to pay is spelt out in the placenames of Suicide Pass, Coffin Canyon, Funeral Peak and Poison Spring.

Here where the mastodons once roamed, men set up their shacks against the elements, to search for riches, but more found death, of which their epitaphs may be still found scratched in the barren rocks.

'A VICTIM OF THE ELEMENTS' reads one epitaph in Death Valley on the isolated grave of Val Nolan, whose life and lonely death in 1931 still remains a Californian mystery. The marker on Nolan's grave was set up by the Park Service after the original had been stolen as a souvenir.

For something to do the prospectors down Desolation Canyon way, Death Valley, used to collect epitaphs. The originals now long erased by sandstorm and landslide, some of these epitaphs still remain in memory thanks to the prospectors who could write noting them down in their diaries. Here are some from an old goldminer's logbook, which show that even in Death Valley humour could still be found:

MARTHA MAYS OF THE GOLD NUGGET SALOON

Here lies the body of Martha Mays
Who was so virginal in stays,
She lived to the age of three score and ten
And gave to the worms what she refused to the men.

YOUNG ABE LOUTH

Here lies the body of Young Abe Louth
Who died of an ornery wisdom tooth.

WHISKY JOE

He had some faults
And many merits
He died of drinking
Home brewed spirits

ANDY MONNEY'S WIFE

Here lies my poor wife,
A bitch and a shrew
If I said I missed her
I should lie too.

HANNAH'S THREE IN A ROW

This old rock has drunk a widow's tear
Three of my husbands are buried here.

COOKHOUSE JAKE

Peace to his hashes.

YIPPEE, I'M FREE!

Pete Connor wrote this of his wife Nancy:

Who far below in this grave doth rest
She's join'd the army of the blest;
The Lord has ta'en her to the sky,
The saints rejoice, and so do I.

FAT MAY PRESTON

Here lies the body of
Fat May Preston
Who's now moved to heaven
To relieve the congestion.

JOB THE ITINERANT ACTOR

Restin'

UNLUCKY BILL SMEE

Here lies Wild Bill Smee
Who ran for sheriff in '83
He also ran in '84
But ain't a runnin' any more!

JOHN SMITH OF SANTA DIGGINGS, CALIFORNIA

In memory of John Smith, who met Wierlent
Death near this ole spot
18 hundert and 40 too. He was shot with his
Own .42
It warrn't one o' them noo fangl't kind
But one o' them with brass knobs and an ole kind o' barrel.
Such is the Kingdom of Heaven.

CHARLOTTE THE HARLOT OF COPPERSTONE CREEK

Here lies the bones of Copperstone Charlotte
Born a virgin, died a harlot.
For sixteen whole years she kep' her virginity
A darn'd long time in this vicinity.

APPLY WITHIN

Here lies the body of Henry Oakes, gunslinger.
If not, notify Chantry & Son, Undertakers, at once.

RHYMIN' PETE

Living and dying I loved the truth
And I'll speak it now, though it seem uncouth;
I wrote thirty poems, and was published as well,
So I don't care now if it's Heaven or Hell!

LARRY THE LUSH

Here lie the earthly remains of
Larry G. Chappell
He hath joined the spirits
Of which he was always so fond.

PERCY THE PRETTY BOY

The mortal remains of Percy Claud Crintle
Lie in the dust under this old lintle.
He worked with us all without any shame
And all he had left was his pretty name.

A ballad of the 1840s 'Sweet Betsy from Pike' gave a vivid picture of the troubles and occasional pleasures of the early travellers westward. Sweet Betsy and Long Ike, her lover, had their home in north-east Missouri, so Californians tagged settlers from the Midwest as 'Pikes' (whether they came from Missouri or not). Among the graveboards 'Unknown', 'Maiden's grave—cholera, aged 21', and 'Jus' loafin' a while', to break the monotony, some 'old timers' had for their epitaphs plays on the rhyme of Sweet Betsy:

Did you ever hear tell of Sweet Betsy from Pike,
Who crossed the wide prairies with her lover Ike,
With two yoke of cattle and one spotted hog,
A tall Shanghai rooster and an old yaller dog?

Ah know'd them maself on the ole wagon train,
For we came from Missouri our fortunes to claim.
But now I'm a-restin' out here or about
'Goodbye, I'm at peace now, I'm glad I backed out!'

Of all Death Valley's ghost towns, the most ambitious and meteoric (the town boomed in 1904 to over 10,000 inhabitants) was Rhyolite, Nevada, which is just outside the Death Valley National Monument's north-eastern boundary. Named after the silica-rich rock, Rhyolite, owes its fame to Ed Cross and

Shorty Harris, whose fabulous 'Bullfrog' strike set off the boom. Although Shorty soon spent his new-found riches his epitaph, written with humour, remains; Here lies Shorty Harris, a single blanket jackass prospector.

For centuries people all over Europe have been buried outside churchyards for a number of reasons, mostly sentimental. There was the old French vagabond who wanted to be buried along the highway he had walked many times during his life (*La nostalgie de la boue*—Homesickness for the gutter), the German soldier who wished to be buried on the battlefield where he had lost so many buddies (*Die gesunden Knochen eines einzigen pommerschen Musketiers*—the healthy bones of a single Pomeranian grenadier), the English shepherd who preferred to be buried on the fells among his flocks, and the American farmer who wanted to remain in a field he had planted since boyhood and the many retired folk who spent so many years in their gardens that they wished to be buried there.

Sometimes, however, burials took place in unusual locations for different reasons.

The plague cast its noxious shadow over Perth, Scotland, in 1665, when deaths rose at an alarming rate. Many folk sought refuge in more rural parts and two girls, Mary Gray and Bessie Bell, close friends from childhood, were among their number. With only a few bare essentials in their pack, the girls walked to the place called Methven (a few miles north-west of Perth) and built themselves a retreat. Unfortunately a visiting friend infected them with the virulent pestilence and the two girls died and were buried together at Dronach Haugh, on the banks of the river Almond; as the old ballad relates:

They thought to lie in Methven Kirk	*church*
Amang their noble kin	*among*
But they maun lie on Lyn(e)doch brae	*must: river-bank*
To beek fornent the sun	*bathe; facing*
O Bessie Bell and Mary Gray	
They were twa bonnie lassies	*two lovely girls*
They biggit a bower on yon burn-brae	*built: that stream*
And theekit it o'er wi rashes	*thatched it over with rushes*

Today this grave is on private land (on the Mansfield Estate near the hamlet of Pitcairngreen) and the spot was railed at a later date than the burial by one of the Lord Lynedochs, who set up the epitaph: *They lived—they loved—they died*—in allusion to the old tale that the girls were in love with the same man.

Half-way between Harleston and Redenhall Church in Norfolk, England, lies Lush's Bush fabled as the site of a suicide's grave. Once it was the practice to bury suicides in the north part of a church (see: *A Book of Epitaphs*. 1967 & 69, *A Book of Superstitions*, 1970. David & Charles/Taplinger Inc.) or even deny them the right of a Christian burial. Some records show that this was the site of multiple graves.

Usually the cadavers of suicides were laid facing west and on occasions facing downwards; not uncommon, too, was the custom (prohibited by an Act of Parliament in 1823) of driving a stake through the suicide's heart (cf. vampirism) to stop them from mystically 'walking'. Today an eye-witness account exists of the last burial to take place hereabouts (in 1813) of a woman who poisoned herself after being accused of infanticide:

> Creeping between the legs of the men standing around the open grave in the gloom of evening a young boy saw the parish constable fix the stake in position, while another drove it home with a heavy (hammer). 'Mr Oldeshaw (the Rector) sitting on his horse in silent charge of the proceedings.

Against the masonry of an old railway bridge near Moor Row, Cumberland, England, lies this inscription of one John Garner (1631-1706), a pastor, who was buried in this unusual Baptist burial ground, now almost entirely hidden under the railway embankment:

> Hear doath the body of John Garner lays
> Who was faithful to the Lord in all his days:
> Who did this burying place freely bestow,
> And dispensed the Gospel without charge you know,
> Unto the people over which he was ordained,
> A pastor unto them he did still remain.
> Buried ye 2 day of December, 1706, aged 75 years.

On the lawn of Rowland Hazard's (of the famous Rhode Island family) house at Peacedale, in Narragansett, Rhode Island, USA, there is a blue stone on which this epitaph was carved; it refers to the strength of one Geoffrey Hazard, called 'Stout Jeffrey', a man of Herculean strength:

> Stout Jeffrey Hazard lifted this Stone,
> In pounds just sixteen twenty one,
> In South Kingston he lived and died,
> God save us all from sinful pride.

The spirit of the nursery rhyme and the local rhyme combined, pervades the epitaph from time to time (a form of folk rhyme in which New England seems to abound), and a popular one comes from Searsport, Maine:

> Under the sod, and under the trees,
> Here lies the body of Solomon Pease.
> The Pease are not here, there's only the pod—
> The Pease shelled out and went to God.

They still call him 'Old Jimmy Garlick', but no one knows his real name, and for more years than any living man can tell his last resting place has been a cupboard in the church of St James Garlickhythe, near Upper Thames Street, London.

'Old Jimmy' first became a personality back in 1666 when the Great Fire of London gutted the church of St James, for among the smouldering ruins was found the embalmed body of this mystery man. His cadaver had been buried in a glass coffin under the high altar, but all papers and funeral bric-à-brac relating to his identity had been, presumably, burnt—and, ever since, the pious and the curious have wondered just who he was.

Again in 1942 'Old Jimmy' made a miraculous escape, when the church received a direct bomb hit. Thereafter 'Old Jimmy' was still to be seen in his glass-fronted case to scare the daylights out of people who come across him unawares.

Some twenty years ago an elderly lady visited the church

and told one of the church officers that she had found out from an old book who 'Old Jimmy' was, and she promised to return with the book the following Sunday—she was never seen again! The superstitious believe that 'Old Jimmy' prefers his anonymity and will do almost anything to protect it!

Some Strange Requests

In Tolleridge Churchyard, near Barnet, Hertfordshire, this slab to an unknown woman reveals how people once gave much thought to 'last requests':

> She repeatedly prayed to be evicted
> For twenty-nine years she was afflicted
> And it was her wish to be buried
> Beneath this ancient tree.

While the Victorians really made a 'spectacle' and an 'occasion' of the funeral, with people like the Rev. Patrick Brontë (father of the famous Charlotte, Emily, Anne and Patrick Branwell Brontë) requesting to be buried in layers of charcoal, the 'last requests' of others seem today to be even more strange.

Major Peter Labillière for instance, expressly desired to be interred on Box Hill, near Dorking, Surrey, in a grave ten feet deep, and the coffin let down in perpendicular fashion. The major's concern to be thus placed was that he would 'come right at last' if 'the world should turn topsy-turvy'.

Another 'standing up' grave of note came about by different circumstances.

Too poor to pay for a normal grave space Ben Jonson (1573-1637), a friend of Shakespeare and one of the great poets and dramatists of his day, was buried upright in the north aisle of Westminster Abbey, with a small square stone to mark the area covered by his coffin. Originally the stone was unlettered until a devotee, one Jack Young, donated 1/6 (18 cents) to a mason to carve the epitaph—O RARE BEN JOHNSON—unfortunately the mason couldn't spell!

A fig tree in the cemetery at Watford, Hertfordshire, represents quite a different request. One account of the tale tells how an atheist, when dying, ordered a fig to be placed in his mouth when he was buried, saying if there really was a God the fig would grow. In time all the faithful around were not surprised when the tombstone split in all directions to allow the fig tree to emerge.

Hughenden Churchyard, near High Wycombe, Buckinghamshire, contains another relic of a strange request:

DIED AT HIGH WYCOMBE, BUCKS
ON THE 24TH MAY, 1837
MR JOHN GREY
AGED 64.

On the marble slab placed on the lid of the coffin was:

HERE WITHOUT NAIL, OR SHROUD, DOTH LIE
OR COVERED BY A PALL, JOHN GREY
BORN MAY 17TH, 1773
DIED—24TH, 1837

In coffin made without a nail,
Without a shroud his limbs to hide
For what can pomp or show avail,
Or velvet pall, to swell the pride?
Here lies JOHN GREY beneath this sod,
Who loved his friends, and fear'd his God.

A contemporary source explains: 'The grave and coffin were made under Mr Grey's own directions more than a year before his death; the inscription on the tablet, and the lines on the gravestone were his own composition, and he gave all orders respecting his funeral himself, the sum of 5s (60 cents) being wrapped in separate pieces of paper for each of the bearers. The coffin was of singular beauty and neatness of workmanship, being apparently more like a piece of drawing-room furniture than a receptacle for the dead'.

Not to be outdone by any cipher writers Prince Silo caused the following strange epitaph to be erected over his tomb. The epitaph, at San Salvador, Oviedo, N Spain, which may be read some 270 different ways from the central S, spells out *Silo Princeps Fecit* (made by Prince Silo):

T I C E F S P E C N C E P S F E C I T
I C E F S P E C N I N C E P S F E C I
C E F S P E C N I R I N C E P S F E C
E F S P E C N I R P R I N C E P S F E

Elsewhere on the tomb were the letters H E S S S S T L, which were decipherable as *Hic est Silo situs, sit sibi terra levis*—Here Silo is buried, may the earth be light upon him.

A youth who died from an excess of fruit pie, requested that the cause of his end be engraved on stone as an example to others—his epitaph is in Monmouth Churchyard, Monmouth:

Currants have check't the current of my blood,
And berries brought me to be buried here;
Pears have par'd off my body's hardihood,
And plumbs and plumers spare not one so spare.
Fain would I feign my fall! so fair a fare

Lessens not hate, yet 'tis a lesson good.
Gilt will not long hide guilt, such thinwashed ware
Wears quickly and its rude touch soon is rued.
Grave on my grave some sentence grave and terse,
That lies not as it lies upon my clay,
But in a gentle strain of unstrained verse,
Prays all to pity a poor patty's prey
Rehearses I was fruitful to my hearse,
Tells that my days are told, and soon I'm toll'd away.

London cemeteries and churches, too, have their own crop of strange requests.

In Hammersmith Church was to be seen the marble monument and epitaph to Sir Nicholas Crispe. After a lifetime of service to his king (Charles I) Sir Nicholas wished his heart to be buried at the feet of his master; so, while the body of Sir Nicholas lies outside the church, his heart was to be found in an urn below the bust of his monarch. On each anniversary of its entombment, for a hundred years, the heart was removed and refreshed with a glass of wine.

Jeremy Bentham (1748-1832), 'one of the most influential men who ever lived', and the founder of Utilitarianism, a school of moral philosophy in which the ethic of the greatest possible happiness for the largest possible number of people was propounded, shocked the people of his time by suggesting that the conventional form of burial be discontinued. In its place Bentham averred that the cadavers of the deceased be preserved, and varnished against the weather, to be set up like statues in the gardens of their former homes as a permanent memorial.

The accomplished writer, chemist, botanist and musician, took steps during his lifetime to, at least, be among the first to undergo this funeral custom. His skeleton, wearing his own clothes, and surmounted by a replacement wax head (the original is still preserved at University College, London) still sits in a cupboard of the University he helped to found.

In the church of St Mary Aldermary, in the City of London, is an ornate memorial with a blank epitaph space, erected by an anonymous mourner. It is said to have been ordered by a widow for her late husband, but before she could compose a suitable epitaph she remarried and forgot all about it!

Although he has been dead nearly three hundred years, the textbook *The Compleat Angler, or the Contemplative Man's Recreation* of Izaak Walton (1593-1683) is still a 'must' for all pursuing angling. There is no monument to Walton in Westminster Abbey, but some years before his death Walton inscribed his own humble epitaph prematurely. On the west wall of the south trancept of Westminster Abbey may be seen the memorial of Isaac Casubon, a friend of Walton, and on this memorial Walton carved, IW 1658.

Fixed to the railings round a tomb in the churchyard of St John's, Hackney, is a small metal tablet with the epitaph:

HEREBY WAS SEEN FOR MANY YEARS BLIND FRED
A SUNNY SOUL

Beneath is a row of raised dots which spell out in Braille:

ONE THING I KNOW; WHEREAS I WAS BLIND, NOW I DO SEE

Another who wished to leave a testament of courage to those who might be downhearted by infirmity, was Lucy Warner who was buried at St Giles Churchyard, Camberwell. Her epitaph reads:

THE LITTLE WOMAN OF PECKHAM
WHO DIED IN 1821 AGED 71

The strange story being that Lucy kept a school where all the children were taller than she was—this teacher measured only 32 inches high!

More often than not it was difficult to have one's own wish concerning a last resting place what with parish, civic and county rules and regulations. Sometimes there was some degree of rivalry as to who had which place of burial, especially in a church. The English poet Robert Browning (1812-89) mirrored this rivalry charmingly in his *The Bishop Orders His Tomb in*

St Praxed's Church, of which this is an extract:

> And so, about this tomb of mine. I fought
> With tooth and nail to save my niche, ye know:
> —Old Gandolf cozened me, despite my care;
> Shrewd was the snatch from out the corner South
> He graced his carrion with, God curse the same!
> Yet still my niche is not so cramped but thence
> One sees the pulpit o' the epistle side,
> And somewhat of the choir, those silent seats,
> And up into the aery dome where live
> The angels, and a sunbeam's sure to lurk:
> And I shall fill my slab of basalt there,
> And 'neath my tabernacle take my rest,
> With those nine columns round me, two and two,
> The odd one at my feet ...
> Peach-blossom marble all, the rare, the ripe
> As fresh-poured red wine of a mighty pulse
> —Old Gandolf with his paltry onion-stone,
> Put me where I may look at him! ...
> And then how shall I lie through centuries,
> And hear the blessed mutter of the mass,
> And see God made and eaten all day long,
> And feel the steady candle-flame, and taste
> Good strong thick stupefying incense-smoke! ...

An epitaph which caused scholars some difficulty in translating was that of the burial-place of King Uzziah, King of Judah in the eighth century BC.

Because the king suffered latterly from leprosy (although the Bible reference of his reign II *Kings* XV gives no reason for his affliction, II *Chronicles* XXV says that he was thus striken down with leprosy for his attempt to usurp priestly functions) he had been confined to his room in the palace. Originally buried in the Citadel of David, his bones were (perhaps) removed from the royal grave because of his disease.

Which means: 'Hither were brought the bones of Uzziah, King of Judah, do not open.' The epitaph stone is now a part of the collection in the Russian Church on the Mount of Olives, Israel.

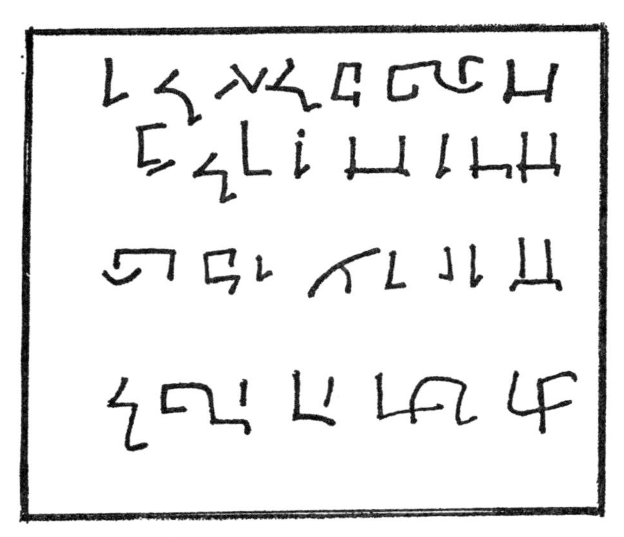

The dirge epitaph in memory of Miss Ellen Gee of Kew, Surrey, offers an easier interpretation:

Peerless yet hapless maid of Q,
Accomplish'd L N G,
Never again shall I and U
Together sip our T.
For, ah! the fates I know not Y,
Sent 'midst the flowers a B,
Which ven'mous stung her in the I,
So that she could not C.
L N exclaim'd Vile spiteful B,
If ever I catch U
On jess'mine, rosebud or sweet P,
I'll change your stinging Q.
I'll send you, like a lamb or U
Across the Atlantic C,
For our delightful Village Q,
To distant O H I E.
A stream runs from my wounded I,
Salt as the briny C,
As rapid as the X or Y,
The O I O or D.
Then fare-thee-well, insatiate B
Who stung nor yet knew Y,
Since not for wealthy Durham's C
Would I have lost my I.
They bear with tears fair L N G
In funeral R A,
A clay-clod corse now doom'd to B
While I mourne her D K.
Ye nymphs of Q, then shun each B
List to the reason Y;
For should a B C U at T,
He'll surely sting U R I
Now in a grave L deep in Q,
She's cold as cold can B,
Whilst robins sing upon A U
Here dirge and L E G.

Poets and the Epitaph

There is hardly a major poet throughout the history of literature who has not at one time or another tried out his skill on the epitaph, both in its verse and prose forms. The following is a representative sample from the literary archives of the English speaking peoples, showing the many different fashions and styles over some four hundred years.

WILLIAM CAMDEN, 1551-1623, celebrated English antiquary and topographer.

My friend, judge not me,
Thou seest I judge not thee.
Betwixt the stirrup and the ground
Mercy I asked, mercy I found.

Remains. Epitaph for a Man Killed by Falling from His Horse.

SIR WALTER RALEIGH, c. 1552-1618. Elizabethan courtier, scholar, soldier and statesman.

Here lies the noble Warrior that
never blunted sword;
Here lies the noble Courtier that
never kept his word;
Here lies his Excellency that
govern'd all the state
Here lies the Lord of Leicester that
all the world did hate.

Epitaph for Robert Dudley, Earl of Leicester, 1531-88.[1]

Even such is time, which takes in trust
Our youth, our joys, and all we have,
And pays us but with age and dust,
Who in the dark and silent grave,
When we have wandered all our ways,
Shuts up the story of our days.
And from which earth, and grave, and dust,
The Lord shall raise me up, I trust.

Written the night before his execution. Found in his Bible in the Gate House at Westminster, London.

BEN(JAMIN) JONSON, 1572-1637 (q.v.)

Would'st thou heare what man can say
In a little? Reader, stay.
Under-neath this stone doth lye
As much beautie, as could dye:
Which in life did harbour give
To more vertue, then doth live.
If, at all, shee had a fault
Leave it buryed in this vault.
One name was ELIZABETH
Th' other let it sleepe with death:
Fitter, where it dyed, to tell
Then that it liv'd at all. Farewell.

On Elizabeth, L. H.

[1] This favourite of Queen Elizabeth I was a soldier and statesman; the epitaph sums up popular contemporary feeling about Leicester.

Weep with me, all you that read
  This little story:
And know for whom a tear you shead
  Death's self is sorry.
'Twas a child that so did thrive
  In grace and feature,
As Heaven and Nature seem'd to strive
  Which own'd the creature.
Years he number'd scarce thirteen
  When Fates turn'd cruel,
Yet three fill'd Zodiacs had he been
  The stage's jewel;
And did act, what now we moan,
  Old men so duly,
As sooth the Parcae thought him one,
  He play'd so truly.
So, by error, to his fate
  They all consented;
But viewing him since, alas, too late!
  They have repented:
And have sought (to give new birth)
  In baths to steep him;
But being so much too good for earth,
  Heaven vows to keep him.

An Epitaph on Salathiel Pavy, a Child of Queen Elizabeth's Chapel.

WILLIAM BROWNE, 1591-1643, poet, from Tavistock, Devon.

Underneath this sable herse
Lyes the subject of all verse:
Sydney's sister, Pembroke's Mother:
Death, ere thou hast slaine another
Faire, and Learn'd, and good as she,
Time shall throw a dart at thee.

Epitaph on the Countess Dowager of Pembroke, died 1621[1]

[1] Authorship of this epitaph was long attributed to Ben Jonson (q.v.)

SAMUEL JOHNSON, 1709-84, the great lexicographer and writer.

Olivarii Goldsmith, Poetae, Physici, Historici
Qui nullum fere scribendi genus non tetigit
Nullum quod tetigit non ornavit.

(To Oliver Goldsmith, A Poet, Naturalist, and Historian, who left scarcely any style of writing untouched, and touched nothing that he did not adorn.)

Epitaph on Oliver Goldsmith. 22 June 1776.

DAVID GARRICK, 1717-79, leading tragic actor of his time.[1]

Here lies Nolly Goldsmith, for shortness call'd Noll,
Who wrote like an angel, but talk'd like poor Poll.

Impromptu Epitaph of Oliver Goldsmith

[1] for Garrick's own epitaph and his epitaph of William Hogarth, the painter, see p 49 *A Book of Epitaphs* (ibid).

WILLIAM WORDSWORTH, 1770-1850, chief among the 'Lake Poets'.

Art thou a Man of purple cheer?
A rosy Man, right plump to see?

A Poet's Epitaph

SAMUEL TAYLOR COLERIDGE, 1772-1834, one of the great English poets whose *Ancient Mariner* (and other poems) stands unsurpassed for poetic beauty and originality.

Ere ain could blight or sorrow fade,
Death came with friendly care:
The opening bud to Heaven convey'd,
And bade it blossom THERE.

On an Infant

THOMAS BABINGTON MACAULAY, BARON MACAULAY, 1800-59, most brilliant historian of the Victorian era.

To my true king I offer'd free from stain
Courage and faith; vain faith and courage vain.
For him I threw lands, honours, wealth away
And one dear hope, that was more prized than they.
For him I languish'd in a foreign clime,
Grey-hair'd with sorrow in my manhood's prime;
Heard on Lavernia Scargill's whispering trees

And pined by Arno[1] for my lovlier Tees;[2]
Beheld each night my home in fever'd sleep,
Each morning started from the dream to sleep;
Till God, who saw me tried too sorely, gave
The resting-place I ask'd, an early grave.
O thou, whom chance leads to this nameless stone,
From that proud country which was once my own,
By those white cliffs I never more must see,
By that dear language which I spake like thee,
Forget all feuds, and shed one English tear
O'er English dust. A broken heart lies here.

A Jacobite's Epitaph[3]

GEORGE MEREDITH OM, 1828-1909, novelist and poet of rich imagination, wit and characterisation.

The Man of England circled by the sands.

Epitaph for Gordon of Khartoum[4]

SIR HENRY JOHN NEWBOLT, 1862-1938, Controller of Wireless in WW I, author and poet remembered for his stirring sea poems.

Foremost of all on battle's fiery steep
Here VERTUE fell, and here he sleeps his sleep,
A fairer name no Roman ever gave
To stand sole monument on Valour's grave.

On Spion Kop—1900[5]

RUDYARD KIPLING, 1865-1936, poet, novelist and miscellaneous writer, well known for his sketches of life in India.

I could not look on Death, which being known,
Men led me to him, blindfold and alone.

Epitaphs of War. The Coward

[1] Arno: river of Central Italy, flows past Florence and Piza.

[2] Tees: river of North England, flows from the Pennines east to the N Sea.

[3] Jacobite: adherent of the Stuart cause after the abdication of King James II.

[4] Major-General George Gordon CB, 1833-85, murdered at Khartoum by the Mahdi's forces.

[5] A hill in Natal, Republic of South Africa, scene of a famous Boer War conflict.

JOSEPH HILAIRE PIERRE BELLOC, 1870-1953, poet, essayist and historian.

It did not last; the Devil howling 'Ho!
Let Einstein be!' restored the status quo.
Answer to Pope's Epitaph for Sir Isaac Newton[1]

ALFRED EDWARD HOUSMAN, 1859-1936, English poet and eminent classical scholar.

These, in the day when heaven was falling,
The hour when earth's foundations fled,
Followed their mercenary calling
And took their wages and are dead.
Their shoulders held the sky suspended;
They stood, and earth's foundations stay;
What God abandoned, these defended,
And saved the sum of things for pay.
Epitaph on an Army of Mercenaries, 1914

FROM ANONYMOUS PENS

Philips, whose touch harmonious could remove
The pangs of guilty pow'r and hapless love,
Rest here, distress'd by poverty no more,
Here find that calm, thou gav'st so oft before.
Sleep, undisturb'd, within this peaceful shrine,
Till angels wake thee, with a note like thine.
An Epitaph upon the celebrated Claudy Philips, Musician, who died very poor. (*Gentlemen's Magazine*, Sept. 1740)

I expect to pass through this world but once. Any good therefore that I can do, or any kindness that I can show to any fellow creature, let me do it now. Let me not defer or neglect it, for I shall not pass this way again.

Attributed to many pens, probably most reliably to Stephen Grellet (1773-1855). Attributed also to Edward Courtenay, Earl of Essex, because of a resemblance of his epitaph. (See, *Literary World*, 15 March 1905).

[1] (1642-1727) Generally acknowledged as the world's greatest scientist.

That we spent, we had:
That we gave, we have:
That we left, we lost:

Epitaph of the Earl of Devonshire (quoted by Edmund Spencer c. 1552-99 in *The Shepherd's Calendar*, May 1.7)

The people of Chichester, Sussex, have good reason to believe that their famous associate William Hayley (1745-1820) may rank among Britain's most famous epitaph writers. A cultivated Whig country gentleman and poet, Hayley left a collection of epitaphs[1] of which these are a representative few:

Of the Poet William Collins 1720-56
A great friend of the poet James Thomson and befriended by Samuel Johnson

Ye who the merits of the dead revere,
Who hold Misfortune sacred, Genius dear,
Regard this tomb, where Collins, hapless name
Solicits Kindness, with a double claim
Though nature gave him, and though science taught
The fire of fancy, and the reach of thought,
Severely doom'd to penury's extreme
He pass'd in madd'ning pain life's fev'rish dream.
While rays of genius only serv'd to show
The thick'ning horror, and exalt his woe
Ye walls that echo'd to his frantic moan
Guard the due records of this grateful stone;
Strangers to him, enamour'd of his lays,
This fond memorial to his talents raise.
For this the ashes of the bard require
Who touch'd the tend'rest notes of Pity's lyre;
Who join'd pure faith to strong poetic powers,
Who, in reviving reason's lucid hours,
Sought on one book his troubled mind to rest,
And rightly deem'd the book of God the best.

[1] See: *The Epitaph Book of William Hayley* (1745-1820) by Noel H. Osborne. The Chichester Papers No. 49, Chichester City Council, 1965. 3/6 (42 cents).

On Agnes Cromwell
Daughter of Admiral Cromwell
Monument in Chichester Cathedral

Beauty and Grace her lovely Form exprest
Superior Charms her lovelier Mind possest
There Truth and Tenderness so us'd to shine
Her Life approach'd so near to Life divine
That she appear'd while this rough Earth she trod
A spotless Temple of the living God.

William Hayley's first wife
Buried at Eartham 1797

If lovely Features and a lofty Mind
Tender as charity as Bounty kind
If these were Blessings that to Life could give
A Lot which makes it Happiness to live
Thou fair Eliza hadst been blest on Earth
But seraphs in Compassion wept thy Birth
For thy deep nervous Woes of wondrous Weight
Love could not heal nor Sympathy relate
Yet pity trusts with hallow'd Truth serene
Thy God oerpays them in a purer Scene
Peace to thy ashes to thy Memory Love
And to thy Spirit in the Realms above
All that from blameless sufferings below
Mortality can hope or angels know.

To Admiral Sir George Murray, KGB
His memorial is in the Naval Chapel of Chichester Cathedral

Hail to thy Scene of consecrated Rest
Thy Toil was Honour—Be thy Memory blest
Lamented Murray dear distinguish'd Name
The Lov'd Copartner in thy Nelson's Fame
With mutual Ardour your bright Course begun
Friendship endear'd the Praise your Valour won
Sussex twas thine to show when Murray died
Maternal Sorrow and maternal Pride;

Benign and brave He grac'd his native Earth
With Christian Virtues and heroic Worth
Love hails Him now in Life's celestial Calm
Grac'd by the Lord of Hosts with Glory's Palm.

In Loving Memory of a Fish

A little way off Highway 55, on the old road between Veteran's Hospital and the Mendota bridge, Illinois, USA, through stone portals, stands a low mound and a white gravestone. On the face of the marker, with its display of red plastic carnations, is this epitaph:

WHISKEY
A GREAT HORSE
A STOUT HEART
1911-1943

Whiskey, the famous US Army Trick Horse, was born in 1911 in Montana and came to Fort Snelling, where there is a road called 'Whiskey Road' in his honour, in a consignment of horses.

From the first the horse was considered untrainable, but one lieutenant, W. B. Hazelrigg, saw potential in this 'dumb critter' and, with patience, taught the horse many a party trick including the contortive jumping through hoops, and also used the beast as a polo mount.

Twenty is the age at which ordinary US Army horses are destroyed, but the men of Fort Snelling became attached to Whiskey and the 'top brass' decided to grant the horse a reprieve and to humanely retire it to pasture. After Whiskey was pensioned off he still appeared occasionally at special performances, with the permission of the US Secretary of War.

A story goes that after being separated from his trainer-friend, Lieutenant Hazelrigg, for some seventeen years, Whiskey recognized him immediately when the officer visited him in 1943. Whiskey died on 31 December 1943 and was buried at Fort Snelling with full military honours.

On the North-West Frontier of India stands the grave of 'high-kicking Bessie-Jane' a mule once used by the British Army. Living for kicks was this mule's philosophy and her epitaph reads:

> This stone is erected in respectful memory
> of Bessie-Jane, one of the liveliest mules
> ever to make a British soldier resort to
> swearing. In her lifetime she kicked two
> colonels, two majors, two captains, three
> lieutenants, five sergeants, eleven
> corporals, eighteen privates and, alas,
> one live grenade. It may truly be said
> that she kicked her way through life and
> into death.

In Manchester, England, there is another famous epitaph to a horse, dated 30 September 1843:

> Fallen from his fellow's side,
> The steed beneath is lying;
> In harness here he died;
> His only fault was dying.

Wordless epitaphs in the form of statues have been erected for the oddest reasons, but next to the immortalisation of horses must rank that of dogs.

Usually the sentiment is 'faithful unto death' as with this epitaph taken from a tablet commemorating Gelert's grave at Beddgelert in Caernarvonshire, North Wales:

> In the 13th century, Llewyllyn, Prince of North Wales, had a palace at Beddgelert. One day he went hunting without Gelert, the faithful hound, who was unaccountably absent. On Llewyllyn's return, the truant, stained and smeared with blood, joyfully sprang to meet his master. The Prince, alarmed, hastened to find his son and saw the infant's cot empty, the bedclothes and floor covered with blood. The frantic father plunged his sword into the hound's side, thinking it had killed his son. The dog's dying yell was answered by a child's cry. Llewyllyn searched and discovered his boy unharmed, but near by lay the body of a mighty wolf which Gelert had slain. The Prince, filled with remorse, is said never to have smiled again. He buried Gelert here. The spot is called Beddgelert.

Outside Shibuya Station in Tokyo, can be found the epitaph and statue of Hachiko, the faithful Akita (one of the most typical of Japanese dogs, a sturdy animal which resembles the husky of Alaska and Canada) who went every morning to the station to wait for his master—the dog continued the vigil long after the master was dead.

A similar 'welcome home' dog story celebrated in an epitaph comes from Italy. Every day for nearly fifteen years, Fido, trotted down to the 'bus stop in the village of Borgo San Lorenzo, near Florence, to meet his master Carlo Soriani, but in 1943 the dog was killed in a bombing raid. So impressed by the dog's faithfulness were the people of Borgo San Lorenzo that they erected a memorial with epitaph to the dog in the village square.

Scotland's capital, Edinburgh, too has its world famous dog epitaph. Erected by Baroness Burdett-Coutts, the drinking fountain with memorial inscription in front of Candlemaker's Hall, Edinburgh, immortalizes the devoted terrier 'Greyfriar's Bobby' who pined to death (1858) on the grave of its master John Gray ('Auld Jock') in the adjacent Greyfriars Churchyard.

'American lovers of Bobby' marked John Gray's grave by a granite stone. So fabled did the story of the devoted little dog become that US movie maker Walt Disney made a full-length colour feature of it.

The dog epitaph has also been used as a centre of public controversy, as was to be seen in the epitaph of a mongrel in London early this century.

Anti-vivisectionists erected an epitaph to the mongrel at Battersea in 1906, with the partisan message that the animal had been 'done to death' in a medical experiment without first being anaesthetised. So controversial did the issue become that there were demonstrations (medical students threatened to 'do the statue to death' with a sledgehammer) in Trafalgar Square and questions were asked in the House of Commons. At length, Battersea Council decided that the memorial must go; the statue and epitaph were smashed in a stoneyard but the controversy raged for some time in the drawing-rooms of the main protagonists.

The late Sir Osbert Sitwell also used the shock tactics of the memorial to make known another point of view. He it was who lent a piece of land at the Derbyshire village of Eckington on which to build a war memorial (World War I). In the form of a cannon, the inscription by Sir Osbert, the memorial read thus:

> This gun has been erected here to remind
> the people of Eckington of the wicked
> folly and waste of war responsible for
> the deaths of many of them, and in the
> hope that its ugliness will frighten the
> children so that they grow up with a
> natural hatred of war and the brutal
> machinery that accompanies it.

This headstone 'In Loving Memory of a fish' stands in a cottage garden at Blockley, Gloucestershire:

> Under this soil the old fish do lie.
> Twenty years he lived and then did die.
> He was so tame, you understand
> He would come to eat out of your hand.
> Died April 30, 1855, aged 20.

Highgate cemetery, London, is strange enough with its memorial in the shape of a grand piano on the grave of a young musician, but the most curious is that of a cat. Said to have belonged to Dick Whittington (c.1358-1423 the wealthy London mercer who was three times mayor of London) the cat statue is thought to mark the place where Dick is supposed to have heard the bells of London calling him to fame and fortune.

At Mount Rushmore, in the Black Hills of Dakota, USA, is the greatest and most stupendous of the world's 'silent epitaphs'; the memorial comprises the 230 ft tall carved busts of America's four greatest presidents, Jefferson, Washington, Lincoln and Theodore Roosevelt, whose detailed faces were hewn by powerdrills after masses of rock had been blasted away.

Perhaps the most curious epitaph in the whole of London was that:

> In Memory of
> ye Cherry Pey
> As cost ½ a Guiney
> ye 17 of July
> That day we had good cheer
> Hope to do so many a Year.
> R.C. 1752 D. Terry

The epitaph from the wall of the George Inn, Wanstead, London, refers to the two men in 1752, who were engaged on repairs to the inn, and who were caught eating a pilfered cherry pie. The magistrate fined them half a guinea ($1.26) and they carved this epitaph to commemorate the event.

Yet the strangest of all epitaphs may yet be built at Eccles, Lancashire, in honour of the cake, first baked some two hundred years ago, that made the town's name famous.

Such a chapter on the epitaphs of fauna cannot be considered complete without a mention of the famous epitaph of Catullus for a sparrow; from *Carmina*:

Lugete, O Veneres Cupidinesque,
Et quantum est hominum venustiorum.
Passer mortuus est meae puellae,
Passer, deliciae meae puellae.

Come, all ye Loves and Cupids, haste
To mourn, and all ye men of taste;
My lady's sparrow, O, he's sped
The bird my lady loved is dead.

What the Butler Didn't See

For many years now those visiting Manor Park cemetery, in London, have been intrigued by this epitaph engraved on a simple marble cross:

Erected to the Memory of
ELIZABETH ANN EVEREST
who died 3rd July 1895
by
WINSTON SPENCER CHURCHILL

And still the questions are murmured as the visitors crunch

off down the path; 'Who was Elizabeth Everest?' 'Was it really *the* Winston Churchill?' 'If so, why did he raise the stone?'

Mrs Elizabeth Ann Everest it seems was the late Sir Winston Churchill's nurse when he was a small boy. Devoted to her, she it was who shared his boyish secrets and, like many a female servant before her, she became as close to her charge as would a mother. Even when he grew up and joined the army Winston Churchill still kept in touch with Mrs Everest, and when in 1895 (Sir Winston was twenty at the time) he learnt that she was gravely ill he went straight to her home to offer what assistance he could.

Sir Winston, seeing how ill Mrs Everest was, called in a London specialist, but it was too late; it was he who arranged his former nurse's funeral and for years thereafter regularly laid flowers on her grave and paid for its upkeep.

In later life Sir Winston once said that if any man honoured him, it was because of the influence of that humble and gentle woman now lying in Manor Park cemetery.

Servants in the past who were devoted to their masters and mistresses, and who knew that their affection was reciprocated, often asked that they might be buried near the vaults of their employers.

King George III so honoured one servant, Mary Gaskoin, aged thirty-one, by erecting a tablet to her memory in St George's Chapel, Windsor, with the words, 'in testimony of his grateful sense of the faithful service and attachment of an amiable young woman to his beloved daughter [*Princess Amelia*], whom she survived only three months' and whose bones were buried 'near this place'.

Many servants' epitaphs were especially written for the edification of other servants, like that of Elizabeth Chapman of Wanstead, of whom it was said that:

By her prudent conduct
And her continuance with great credit
45 years in the same family
She acquired a decent fortune
for the benefit
Of her relations and family.

While one William Cummins of Wickham, Hampshire, fared even better:

And having fulfilled his humble duty
with uprightness and fidelity
for sixty years
bequeathed at his death £800
in gifts of gratitude
and in charity to poor persons in this place
and neighbourhood.

As William Cummins lived in the late 1700s his £800 ($1920) would be then a small fortune.

So impressed by his independence of spirit, the Reverend William Price was inspired to write of his servant Samuel Cane, who died at Epsom, Surrey, in 1782:

He lies a pattern for the human race,
A man who did his work and knew his place ...
In spite of bribes and threats, severely just,
He sought no pension and he broke no trust.

'Knowing one's place' was deemed an excellent quality in a servant, no less in a servant's wife, as can be seen on an epitaph at Streatham:

Elizabeth, wife of Henry Tapsall, manservant to
Lord ——— was married to her spouse some 47 years
and never did one thing to disoblige her husband
———she died in 1746 by his desire.

Magnanimous employers sometimes immortalized their generosity in stone, for on the tombstone of John Quinny for instance, who for fifty-six years was a servant of Sir Henry Chester, of Tilsworth, Bedfordshire, is written:

His master left him an annuity of £8.

Nevertheless shabby treatment did not go unregarded; from a tombstone at Langley Marish, Buckinghamshire:

Sacred to the Memory of
Mrs Sarah Wall
the old and faithful but ill-requited
servant of Lord Carrington
who departed this life June 1832
aged 70 years.

Mrs Wall apparently was not satisfied with the provision the noble lord had made for her, and her executors seemed to share her indignation. The incumbent of the parish ordered the sexton to paint out the words 'but ill-requited', with the rather ironic result that the paint used was so strong that it preserved these words when the weather had almost obliterated the rest!

Ann Arnold, however, of Gloucester, who died in 1760 and was for forty years the servant of one Charles Brerton was able to requite her employers!

Amidst a great corruption of manners in that
class of people she retained an unblemished
simplicity and innocence, discharged her
duty on the genuine and disinterested principals (*sic*)
of affection and Christianity. She ordered
by her will that the little fruits of her labour should
at length return to the family in which she had
earned them and from whom she had deserved
much greater.

Ann's attitude of 'render therefore unto Caesar the things that are Caesar's' was certainly in line with the clause in the last will and testament of the Welsh landowner's butler who left '£5 to buy oil to burn the old b——d's stables'.

Coloured servants too were given marked graves. At Teston, Kent, there is still to be found the tomb of 'Nestor, a black' who died at the age of thirty-six and was buried near his master the Reverend James Ramsay. Nestor's epitaph also included his fate 'By robbers torn from his country and enslaved, he attached himself to his master'.

At Hampton, Middlesex, lies Pompey the coloured servant of Lady Thomas, who 'behaved himself lowly and reverend to all his betters, civil and kind to all his equals'.

Few loved their work as did Elizabeth Gay, however, on whose gravestone is revealed this startling comment:

... who after a service of
40 years
finding her strength diminished
with unparalleled disinterestedness
requested that her wages might
be proportionally lessened.

The Pharaohs of Ancient Egypt seem also to have given some thought to the epitaphs of those who served them. At the funeral of Neferhotep this epitaph was sung:

Be happy then ...
Come, scents and perfumes are set before thee,
Mahu-flowers, and lilies for the arms and neck
Of thy beloved, who dwells in thy heart.
Come, songs and music are before thee.
Cast behind thee all care and mind thee of joy,
Until the day cometh whereon thou shalt go down
Unto the land which loveth silence.

While the precept of the great sage 'Eney might be carved on many a female servant's tomb:

... (she) nourished thee in all manner of ways. If thou forgettest her, she might blame thee, she might 'lift up her arms to God, and He would hear her complaint'. After the appointed months ... she nursed thee for three years. She brought thee up, and when thou did enter the school, and was instructed in the writings, she came daily to thy master with bread and beer from her house.

From time to time employers, like Sir Charles Hanbury Williams, were moved to write expansive epitaphs about their servants in the age old grand manner.

(In Trevethin Churchyard, Monmouth.)

To the memory of
MR THOMAS COOKE,
Agent of the iron-works of Pontypool,
who died August 1st, 1739,
Aged 66 years

With most religious truth it may be said,
Beneath this stone an honest man lies dead.
Vice he abhorred, in virtue's path he trod,
Just to his master, humble to his God.
Useful he lived, and void of all offence,
By nature sensible, well-bred by sense;
His master's interest was his constant end,
(The faithful'st servant, and the truest friend;)
For him his heart and hand were always join'd,
And love with duty strictly was combined.
Together through this vale of life they passed,
And in this church together sleep at last;
For when the master's fatal hour was come,
The servant sighed, and followed to the tomb;
And when at the last day he shall appear,
Thus shall his Saviour speak, and scatter fear,
'Well done, thou faithful servant, good and just,
Receive thy well-deserved reward of trust;
Come where no time can happiness destroy
Into the fulness of thy Master's joy'.

The last four lines refer to the quotation from Matthew xxv. 21: 'His Lord said unto him. Well done, thou good and faithful servant: thou hast been faithful over a few things, I will make thee ruler over many things: enter thou into the joy of thy lord.'

A wonderful epitaph indeed but sometimes the quote was unfortunately placed!

From one grave in Gibraltar:

Here lies
Captain Ernest Blomfield
Accidentally shot by his Orderly
March 2nd 1789
'Well done thou good and faithful servant'.

Here are some further epitaph comments on servants of one kind and another:

In the nave of Wing Church, Buckinghamshire, there is a curious brass plate bearing the effigy of a man in a cloak kneeling, with a porter's staff under his feet, a high-crowned hat, and a large key lying behind him. His hands are lifted up as if in prayer, and below is the following inscription:

Honest old THOMAS COTES, that sometimes was
Porter at Ascott Hall[1], hath now (alas!)
Left his key, lodge, fyre, friends, and all to have
A room in Heaven. This is that good man's grave,
Reader, prepare for thine, for none can tell,
But that you two may meet to-night. Farewell.
He died 20th November, 1648.
Set up at the appointment and charges of
his friend GEO HOVGHTON

Dortmund Cemetery, Westphalia, Germany:

Heinrich Bruggeman heissich,
Nach dem Himmel reise ich,
Will mal seh'n Jesus macht,
Liebe Bruder, gute nacht.

On a brass in Arreton Church, Isle of Wight, c.1430, is this example of a servant's epitaph which also forms an early example of the English language:

Here is ybyried under this grave
HARRY HAWLES his soul god save
Longe tyme steward of the yle of wyght
Have m'cy on hym, god ful of myght.

[1] Home of the Dormer family.

For servitor Susan Mum:

To the memory of SUSAN MUM
Silence is wisdom.

Epitaph of a woman who once served ale at the 'Pig and Whistle' Greenwich, 1789:

Assign'd by Providence to rule a tap,
My days past glibly, till an awkward rap,
Some way, like bankruptcy impell'd me down.
But up I got again and shook my gown
In gameson gambles, quite as brisk as ever,
Blithe as the lark and gay as sunny weather;
Composed with creditors, at five in pound,
And frolick'd on till laid beneath this ground.
The debt of nature must, you know, be paid,
No trust from her—God grant extent in aid.

Epigrammatic Epitaphs

In the course of time the epigram has come to mean any pithy (and usually pungent) saying in prose or verse, but its original meaning of 'an inscription' made the literary form popular with epitaph writers, monumental masons, and those looking for something 'classical' for their last memorial.

The verse epigram is one of the most catholic of literary forms, and lends itself to the expression of almost any kind of feeling or thought. S. T. Coleridge placed in verse form an epigram on what he thought the epigram should contain:

What is an Epigram? a dwarfish whole,
Its body brevity, and wit its soul.

(Also mentioned Brander Matthews' *American Epigrams. Harper's Magazine Nov., 1903*)

Whilst an unknown writer averred:

The qualities rare in a bee that we meet,
In an epigram never should fail—

The body should always be little and sweet,
And a sting should be left in its tail.

Echoed by the Latin scholar Martial who put it another way:

Omne epigramma sit instar apis; sit aculeus illi
Sit sua mella; sit et corporis exiguli.
Three things must Epigrams, like bees, have all,
A sting, and honey, and a body small.

The epigram, of which the epitaph is a variety, was much cultivated in Greece because of that nation's love of the brief and well pointed argument, and the pattern set by Simonides (556-468 BC) in his lines on those who fell at Thermopylae in 490 BC during the conflict between the Persians and the Greeks, has perhaps never been betterd:

ὦζεῖν', ἄγγειλον Λακεδαιμονίοις ὅτιτῆδε,
κείμεθα, τοῖς κείνων ῥήμαοι πειθόμενοὶ.
Tell the Spartans, thou that passest by,
Here in obedience to their word we lie.
(J. W. Mackail. *Select Epigrams from the Greek Anthology*)

Following on, the tricliniums of Ancient Rome once rang with the (often bawdy) epigrams of such famous writers as Catullus.

Gratias tibi maximas Catullus
Agit pessimus omnium poeta,
Tanto pessimus omnium poeta,
Quanto tu optimus omnium patronum.
Catullus gives you warmest thanks,
And he the worst of poets ranks;
As much the worst of bards confessed,
As you of advocates the best.

In English literature proper there is no writer like Martial or Logau of Germany (*Deutsche Sinngedichte Drey Tausand* 1654) whose fame is entirely due to his epigrams, although

Weever's collection of 1599 (interesting mainly for his allusion to Shakespeare) may have been the catalyst to set the chain of such poets as Herrick, Dryden, Swift, Addison, Johnson, Goldsmith, Burns, Blake, Shelley and Landor writing epigrams, with in some cases great success. In more recent years poets like W. B. Yeats, Hilaire Belloc, and J. C. Squire have been noted for their epigrams.

The French were undoubtedly the most successful with the 'salt and vinegar' epigram like this one from a graveyard at Nantes,

> Beneath this stone a quibbling lawyer lies
> For sixty years who squeezed his neighbour's purses;
> If he can see you now, I'm sure he cries
> That you have paid no fee to read these verses.

while the Germans tended towards the moral and didactic themes.

A selection of Latin epigrams from graveyards at Lucerne, Switzerland, Paris, France, Stockholm, Sweden, Hanover, in the Federal Republic of Germany and Nijmegen, Netherlands show how 'classicism' prevailed: First four after Catullus

> *Qui nunc it per iter tenebricosum*
> *Illuc, unde negant redire quenquam.*
> And now he treads the gloomy track
> Whence no one, so they say, comes back.

> *Sed haec prius fuere.*
> All this is over now.

> *Quid est? quid moraris emori?*
> How now? why not be quick and die?

> *Desine de quoquam quicquam bene velle mereri*
> *Aut aliquem fieri posse putare pium.*
> Cease to expect to win men's gratitude.
> To think that human beings can be grateful.

While these are obviously culled from Martial's *Epigrammata*:

Non est, crede mihi, sapientis dicere 'Vivam':
Sera nimis vita est crastina: vive hodie
It sorts not, believe me, with wisdom to say 'I shall live'.
Too late is to-morrow's life; live thou to-day.

Sunt bona, sunt quaedam mediocria, sunt mala plura
Quae legis hic: (aliter non fit, Avite, liber.)
There are good things, there are some indifferent, there are more things bad than you read here.
(Not otherwise, Avitus, is a book produced.)

Bonosque
Soles effugere atque abire sentit,
Qui nobis pereunt et imputantur.
And he feels the good days are flitting and passing away, our days that perish and are scored to our account.

Non est vivere, sed valere vita est.
Life is not living, but living in health.

Others favouring alternative Latin writers:

Balnea, vina, Venus corrumpunt corpora nostra;
Sed vitam faciunt balnea, vina, Venus.
Baths, wine, and Venus cause our bodies to decay:
But baths, wine, and Venus make up the sum of life.
(i.e., Wine, women and warmth against our lives combine,
But what were life without warmth, women and wine.)

Corpus omne sive arescit in pulverem,
Sive in humorem solvitur,
Vel in cinerem comprimitur,
Vel in nidorem tenuatur,
Subducitor nobis; sed Deo elementorum custode reservatur.
(When death happens) every body is reduced to dust,

dissolved into fluid, converted to ashes, or wasted away by evaporation, and so withdrawn from our sight; but it is preserved in the hands of God, the guardian of the elements.

The European nations also favoured epigrams from the Greek for their gravestones:

The man who first laid down the pedant rule
That love is folly, was himself a fool;
For if to life that transport you deny,
What privilege is left us—but to die?

(Rome)

To stone the gods have changed her—but in vain—
The sculptor's art has made her breathe again.

(A German graveyard epigram taken from the Greek inscription on the Statue of Niobe, daughter of Tantalus, king of Lydia.)

Found on a lawyer's tomb in Belgium:

A plaintiff thus explained his cause
To counsel learned in the laws:—
'My bondmaid lately ran away,
And in her flight was met by A——
Who, knowing she belonged to me,
Espoused her to his servant B——.
The issue of this marriage, pray,
Do they belong to me or A——?'
The lawyer, true to his vocation,
Gave sign of deepest cogitation;
Look'd at a score of books, or near,
Then hemm'd, and said, 'Your case is clear;
Those children so begot by B——,
Upon your bondmaid, must, you see,
Be yours, or A——'s; —now, this I say,
They can't be yours if they to A——
Belong;—it follows then, of course,
That if they are not his, they're yours.
Therefore, by my advice, in short
You'll take the opinion of the court.'

While in Britain the tombstone epigrams were somehow reflective of the deceased's occupation, name or personage.

A DOCTOR OF THEOLOGY

You tell us, Doctor, 'tis a sin to steal;
We to your practice from your text appeal.
You steal a sermon, steal a nap; and pray
From dull companions don't you steal away?

ON A CHILD (*after Alexander Pope*)

Behold the child, by Nature's kindly law,
Pleased with a rattle, tickled with a straw;
Some livelier plaything gives his youth delight,
A little louder, but as empty quite;
Scarfs, garters, gold, amuse the riper sage,
And beads and prayer-books are the toys of age;
Pleased with this bauble still, as that before,
Till tired he sleeps, and life's poor play is o'er.

EPIGRAM FOR A DECEASED RAILWAY GUARD

Short was his passage through this earthly vale,
By railway lines where mortals used to wend;
But now he travels by way of heaven's rail,
As soon again to reach his journey's end.

ON MISS FANNY CARELESS

CARELESS by name, and Careless by nature;
Careless of shape, and careless of feature.
Careless in dress, and Careless in air;
Careless of riding in coach or in chair.
Careless of love, and Careless of hate;
Careless if crooked, and Careless if straight:
Careless at table, and Careless in bed;
Careless if maiden, Careless if wed.
Careless at church, and Careless at play;
Careless if company go, or they stay.
E'en Careless at tea, not minding chit-chat;
So Careless! She's Careless for this or for that.
Careless of all love or wit can propose;
She's Careless—so Careless—there's nobody knows.

Oh how could I love thee, I know now thou'rt dead
For here to thy graveside my steps now are led.

OF A MAN THRICE MARRIED

He who marries once may be pardon'd his infirmity;
He who marries twice is mad; but if you should find a fool
Marrying thrice, don't spare the lad,
Flog him, flog him, back to school.

EPIGRAM ON THE TOMB OF A BREWER'S COACHMAN

Here lies honest William, a good natured fellow
Who did far too often get rubicund mellow.
Body-coachman was he to an eminent brewer—
No better e'er sat on a box to be sure.
His coach was kept clean, and no mothers or nurses
Took that care of their babes as he took of his horses.
He had these—ay, and fifty good qualities more,
But the business of tippling could ne'er be got o'er:
So his master effectually mended the matter,
By hiring a man who drank nothing but water.
'Now William' says he, 'you see the plain case,
If you drink as he does then you'll keep your place'.
'Drink water!' quoth William, 'I'd far sooner die'
And now with his ancestors William do lie.

In the United States, they preferred something more poetic or witty:

Our life's a journey in a winter's day;
Some only break their fast, and so away;
Others stay dinner, and depart full fed;
The deepest age but sups and goes to bed.

(Maryland)

To this church I once went,
But I grieved and I sorrowed;
For the season was Lent
And the sermon was borrowed.

(Virginia)

At length my friends the feast of life is o'er;
I've eat sufficient—and I'll drink no more:
My night is come; I've spent a jovial day;
'T is time to part; but oh!—what is to pay?

(Connecticut)

'Call silence!' the Judge to the officer cries;
'This hubbub and talk, will it never be done?
Those people this morning have made such a noise,
We've decided ten cases without hearing one.'

(A judge's grave, Louisiana)

In England, rivers all are males—
For instance, Father Thames.
Whoever in Columbia sails,
Finds them Ma'amselles or Dames;
For there the softer sex presides,
Aquatic, I assure ye:
And Mrs. Sippi rolls her tides
Responsive to Miss.Souri.

(Missouri)

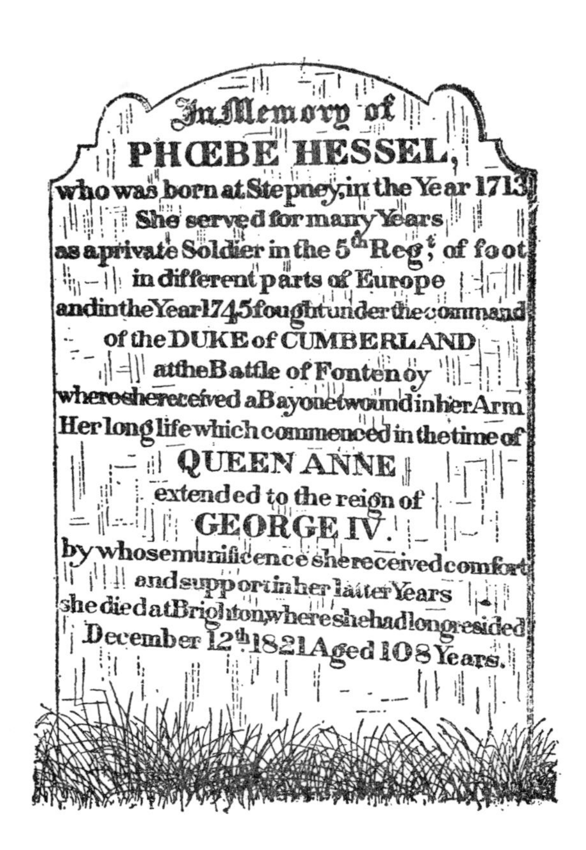

A Triptych of Amazons

THE LADY PUGILIST

Hanslope Churchyard

Strong and athletic was my frame
Far away from home I came
And manly fought with Simon Byrnne
Alas! but lived not to return.

Reader, take warning by my fate
Unless you rue your case too late;

And if you've ever fought before
Determine now to fight no more.

THE SECRET OF LONGEVITY

To the Memory of Sarah Palmer, she departed this life March 1792 in the 91st year of her life

By His kind help, Who sits on Heaven's throne,
I reached the reverenced age of ninety-one,
At eighty-seven I had a broken shin,
At eighty-nine I halved my dose of gin,
And being come to ripe maturity
Plac'd all my thoughts upon futurity,
Thinking I heard a bless'd angel say,
Cheery old soul! pack up and come away.

A FEMALE SERJEANT-MAJOR
Wilhemina Middlehampton of His Majesty's
First foot (& mouth ?)
Died Nov 13, 1834. aged 48

A wife and mother, comrade, friend sincere,
A British soldier brave, lies buried here.
In Spain and Flushing, and at Waterloo,
She fought to guard her country from the foe;
Her comrades, Britons, who survive her, say,
She acted nobly on that glorious day.

Secret Tombs and Charmed Inscriptions

There is a tombstone in the churchyard of St Mary's, Odstock, England, which reads:

IN MEMORY
OF
JOSHUA SCAMP
WHO DIED
April 1st 1801

At one time the tombstone used to have a further inscription:

MAY HIS BRAVE DEED BE REMEMBERED
TO HIS CREDIT, HERE AND HEREAFTER

Joshua Scamp, a gypsy, was wrongfully hanged in Salisbury Gaol for stealing a horse. The real culprit was his son-in-law, but Scamp kept quiet to save the lad. All to no purpose, however, for the young man was hanged six months later for stealing another horse.

Every year after that the gypsies of Joshua Scamp's tribe visited his grave at Odstock. This annual meeting became somewhat rowdy and almost 'sabbatical', so the vicar, the Rev. Grove, his church-warden, Mr Hodden and the church clerk, Mr Hackett, decided to lock the church premises on the next anniversary, and forbid the gypsies entry. They also removed the fence which the gypsies had erected around the grave.

Being denied access to her father's grave, Joshua Scamp's daughter laid the following curse that, 'the man who had done this deed might die; that the church-warden might never prosper; and that the parson might never speak plainly again'.

Within a week Mr Hackett died and the Rev. Grove had a severe stroke which left him with an impediment in his speech: Mr Hodden died within the year!

Thus has the gravestone and epitaph passed into the realm of superstition and the supernatural. The chronicle of belief in life after death runs from the Neanderthal burials of 50,000 years ago to the rise of Spiritualism, which is usually dated from investigations of mysterious noises supposedly made by the spirit of a murdered man, in the house of the Fox family at Hydeville, New York, USA, in the late 1840s. Yet, it was not long in his history that man formulated a cognisance that the 'power' of the dead in their new abode beyond mortality might be harnessed through epitaphs. At first the magic letters were in the form of symbols, like this prehistoric selection from Australia, California, Crete and Italy:

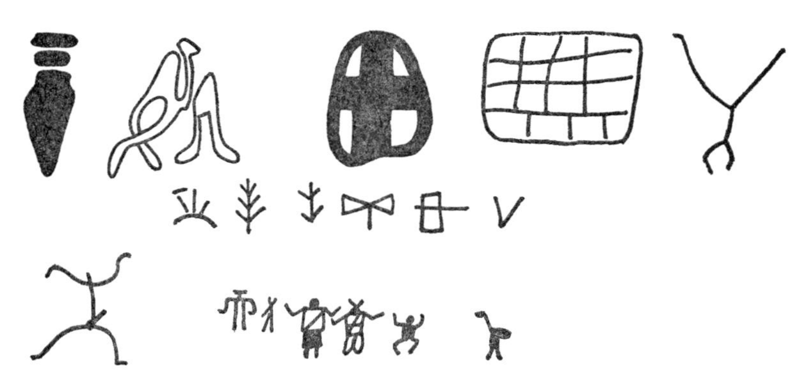

With the coming of the Ancient Egyptians, however, the epitaph developed into more of an incantation to actually try to assist the deceased (a king usually) to join the gods, as the *Book of the Dead* testifies, from a pharaoh's epitaph:

He flieth as a bird, and he settleth as a beetle
on an empty seat that is the ship of Re[1] ...
He roweth in the sky in thy ship, O Re
and he cometh to land in thy ship, O Re.

For centuries it has been a common idea that man is composed of two component parts—a soul (spirit) and a material body; the latter being 'controllable' and the former 'uncontrollable' by man himself. From this idea there grew the superstition, which lasted well into the 1890s both in Europe and the USA, that it was dangerous to tread on or near the grave of a murdered person, lest the spirit of the victim interred below might wreak vengeance on the trespasser.

Thus graves like the following would be avoided:

THE UNFORTUNATE SAILOR,
THURSLEY CHURCHYARD, SURREY
In Memory of
A generous but unfortunate Sailor
Who was barbarously murdered on Hindhead ...
By three Villains
After he had liberally treated them
And promised them his farther Assistance
On the Road to Portsmouth

When pitying Eyes to see my Grave shall come
And with a generous Tear bedew my Tomb
Here shall they read my melancholy Fate
With Murder and Barbarity complete
In perfect Health and in the Flower of Age
I fell a Victim to three Ruffians' Rage
On bended knee I mercy strove to obtain
Then Thirst of Blood made all Entreaties vain
No dear Relation or still dearer Friend

[1] i.e., the Sun God.

Weeps my hard lot or miserable End.
Yet o'er my sad remains—my name unknown—
A generous public have inscribed this stone.

Anxious to allay the sailor's spirit, deemed to wander the earth as all those murdered must, wellwishers had a further epitaph erected at the scene of the crime:

THE SAILOR'S EPITAPH, HINDHEAD, SURREY

ERECTED
In detestation of a barbarous Murder
Committed here on an unknown Sailor
on September 24th 1786
By Edward Lonegon, Michael Casey & James Marshall
Who were taken the same day
And hung in Chains near this place

Whoso sheddeth Man's Blood, by Man shall his
Blood be shed. Gen. Chap: 9 Ver 6.

ROBERT BAXTER, 1796, KNARESDALE, NORTHUMBERLAND

All you that please these lines to read,
It will cause a tender heart to bleed.
I murdered was upon the fell,
And by a man I knew full well.
By bread and butter which he'd laid,
I being harmless, was betrayed.
I hope he will rewarded be
That laid that poison there for me.

Various curses too have been associated with the graves of others who met violent deaths. The story of the 'Robber's Grave'—the grave of the man unjustly hanged, on which no grass will grow—being an example which has intrigued not only the inhabitants of Montgomery, where the grave is situated, but the many visitors from Europe, Australia and the USA who seek it out.

The story goes as follows: During the sessions of 20 April

1821, two magistrates at Welshpool, Montgomeryshire, had before them a John Davies, a plasterer and slaterer of Wrexham, lately working at Oswestry. Davies stood accused by a Welshpool labourer, William Jones, of assaulting him on the road a few miles from Welshpool near Newton, and robbing him of a watch (valued at 30/–, $3.60) and five pennies, on the previous night.

Davies pleaded 'not guilty', but as the prosecution was able to bring two witnesses to testify that the stolen goods were found on Davies's person, the jury found him guilty. Such a robbery in those days, of course, was punishable by death.

According to the records of the time, just before the noose was placed around Davies's neck, on the public scaffold, he was heard by the assembled company to curse his accusers and to pray to God *that He would not allow the grass to grow on his grave as a sign of his innocence*.

Just as this declaration was made, 'the sky', it was said, 'became suddenly overcast and a furious storm of thunder, lightning and rain took place—which convinced many of the bystanders of the truth of the victim's protestations'. (This latter story is corroborated by the weather annals in the *Salopian Journal* for that date).

Davies was buried in Montgomery Churchyard in a part of the ground where there had been no previous burials.

Today this 'cursed' grave, where no grass grows, lies about twenty-four feet west of the path from the north gate of the churchyard to the church tower, and about thirty-six feet from the gate, and is in the form of a simple sunken cross in the ground, amidst the surrounding grass, with a rose bush (planted much later than the burial by a wellwisher—and not by a lover, as fanciful legend has it) near by.[1]

Another grave, once shunned with dread by the superstitious, was that of the 'highwayman' in Wiltshire. A highwayman, so the old story goes, once concealed himself in the trees along a ridge of the downland, half a mile west of the Beckhampton (on the north side of the A361 Swindon-Devises) road. When he rode out of hiding to rob the London-Bath

[1]For a detailed account of this story, its facts, legends and the examining magistrates' depositions see: MONTGOMERYSHIRE COLLECTIONS, Vol 56.1959. pp21-44).

stagecoach, he was shot by one of the guards. Tradition has it that he was buried, face downwards, head pointing west in mystic ritual to allay his spirit, near where he tumbled dead from his horse. Today a sarsen (twenty-one inches in height, ten inches wide and tapering) marks the spot. Some time after there grew the belief that the man shot dead was not a highwayman at all, but a harmless rider; thereafter people kept away from the grave in case *they* be punished by the victim's ghost.

Yet another highwayman seems to have been quite content with his fate, for in his epitaph at Nayland, Suffolk, there is a touch of humour:

My friend, here I am—Death has at last prevailed,
And for once all my projects are baffled.
'Tis a blessing to know, though, when once a man's nailed,
He no longer has fear of the scaffold.

My life was cut short by a shot through the head
On his Majesty's highway at Dalston;
So now 'Number One's' numbered one of the dead.
All's one if he's Alston or all-stone.

(From the grave of Edward Alston 1720-60 the notorious Essex highwayman).

Sometimes the living were afraid that evil forces might assail them when dead, so they left instructions to have a number of mystic symbols and talismanic inscriptions on their tombstones, just in case:

Others, however, relied on 'family luck' to protect them after death. There is a curious tombstone in Moulin Churchyard, in Atholl (extreme north of Perthshire, Scotland) showing the clan Robertson coat-of-arms; a captive man lies below the shield, for the Robertson chiefs have the rare distinction of such an extra 'single supporter' in commemoration of their capture of King James I's (i.e. James I of Scotland) slayer in 1437. Nevertheless beneath the heraldic emblazonment there are the usual symbols of coffin, skull and hourglass, surmounted by a *brideag* figure.

Anchor symbol of
salvation and hope
Europe & E. Coast of USA

A favoured symbol
on
Chinese tombs

Greek mortuary
symbol

Symbol of the soul
European

N. England

Peace for the
dead

Crete Modern
America

The *brideag* (a bat with a human face), also appears on the tombstones of the Fergussons at Strachur, Argyllshire, for a *brideag* is said to flutter eerily at the window of a house when a (Glenshellish) Fergusson is about to die.

Perhaps the most mystically powerful spot in Scotland is Tomnahurich, 'the Knoll of the Yew Wood' in Gaelic, near Inverness, now a double circle of tombstones. Here Simon Fraser, Lord Lovat (1667-1747, a prominent Jacobite) held his Court, for the Frasers held horse-races here as early as 1500. As horse-racing was a pagan religious festival, the custom may have been very ancient, for Tomnahurich was magic ground in the old days. Burt, an English officer writing around 1730 tells that 'the Fairies within it are innumerable, and witches find it the most convenient place for their frolics and gambols in the night-time'. People buried here are thought to be richly rewarded in the afterlife.

Sometimes men's epitaphs are not in written form at all, we have seen, but are unspoken mysteries surrounding their bones. What could account for the peculiar arrangement of some fifty human skeletons found in the caves at Burrington Combe, Somerset, some years ago? The bones formed a circle, with their feet pointing to the centre. Were these cave-men holding some tribal conclave, or just sleeping, when a calamity, sudden as that of Pompeii, overtook them? Speculation is perhaps the only answer. Even today the graves of our ancestors whether in the leafy churchyards of Britain, Germany, France and Italy, or in New England, USA, pose a thousand riddles that defy solution.

Gravestone Backchat

THE ITALIAN BEAUTY

Here lies Estella
who transported a large fortune to heaven
in acts of charity,
and has gone thither to enjoy it.

THE MYSTERY OF MARRIAGE, WELTON, YORKSHIRE

Here lies he, owld Jeremy,
Had seven wives, and eight (sic) times married been;
Now here in his age, he lies in his cage
Under the grass so green.

OF RICHARD AND SUSAN SCATCHERD
South Cave, Welton, Yorkshire

That Dick loved Sue was very true;
Perhaps you'll say, what's that to you
That she loved Dick, and in it's this,
That Dick loved Sue and that made bliss.

TOMBSTONE FROM MIDNAPORE, WEST BENGAL, INDIA

Stop, readers, and lament the loss of a departed beauty,
for here are laid at rest the earthly relicks of
MRS SUSANNA BIRD
who bade a long adieu to
a most affectionate husband and three loved pledges of their
union on the 10th of September, 1784,
aged twenty-four years.

The bird confined within this cage of gloom.
Tho' faded her fine tints, her youthful bloom.
Tho' no soft note drop from her syren's tongue,
By sleep refresh'd, more beauteous gay and young,
Will rise from earth, her seraph's wings display,
And chaunt her anthems to the God of day.

ST PETER'S CHURCH, ISLE OF THANET, KENT

Against his will
Here lies George Hill,
Who from a cliff
Fell down quite stiff.
Where it happened is not known,
Therefore not mentioned on this stone.

ELIZABETH EYRE

the wife of Thomas Eyre, Gent, and daughter of
John Yerbury, Gent, departed this life August 29th, 1637.

Here lies an Heire, who to an Heire was joined,
And dying left a little Heire behind.
Hard-hearted Death, herein was somewhat mild,
Hee tooke the mother, but he spared the child
Yet the one's more happy farre then is the other,
The child's an Heire on Earth, in heav'n the mother,
Where with triumphant Saints and Angells bright,
Shee now enjoyes her blessed Saviour's sight.

THOMAS ALLEYN'S TOMB, WITCHINGHAM

Death here advantage hath of life I spye,
One husband with two wives at once may lye.

ON WILLIAM LEPINE, FAVERSHAM, KENT

Of facetious memory
Ob, the 11th March, 1778
Aet 30 years
Alas.

Where be your jibes now?
Your gambols, your flashes
Of merriment that were wont
To set the Table in a roar.

THE MURDERED THOMAS MANINGLEY

Bromsgrove, Worcestershire, 1817

Beneath this Stone lies the Remain,
Who in Bromsgrove Street was slain.
A Currier with his knife did the deed,
And left me in the street to bleed.
But when Archangel trump shall sound
And souls to bodie join, that Murderer,
I hope shall see my soul in Heaven secure.

A MAN WHO DROVE AN ARMOURED TRAIN AT KIMBERLY

No more will he stand on the footplate,
No more will he steam into town.
He has shut off his steam for ever,
And gone to pick up his crown.

SAGA OF A SEAFARING MAN

Capt. H. Clark, 1836, Bideford Churchyard, N. Devon

Our worthy Friend, who lies beneath this stone
Was Master of a vessel all his own,
Houses and Lands had he, and Gold in Store,
He spent the whole, and would if ten times more.

For twenty years he scarce slept in a bed
Linhays and Limekilns lulled his weary Head,
Because he would not to the Poorhouse go,
For his Proud Spirit would not let him go.

The Blackbirds whistling Notes at break of Day
Used to awake him from his Bed of Hay.
Unto the Bridge and Quay he then repaired,
To see what Shipping up the River Steered.

Oft in the week he used to view the Bay,
To see what Ships were coming in from Sea.
To Captains' Wives he brought the welcome News
And to the Relatives of all the Crews.

At last poor HARRY CLARK was taken ill,
And carried to the Workhouse 'gainst his Will,
But being of this Mortal Life quite tired,
He lived a Month, and then expired.

A PIE-WOMAN OF FOLKESTONE, KENT
To Eleanor Bachelor

Beneath in the dust, the mouldy old crust
Of Nell Bachelor lately was shoven,
Who was skilled in the arts of pies, custards and tarts,
And knew well every use of the oven.
When she lived long enough, she made her last puff,
A puff by her husband much praised,
Now here she doth lie, to make a dirt pie
In hopes that her crust will be raised.

LAMBETH CHURCHYARD

Here lieth W(illiam) W(ilson)
Who never more will trouble you, trouble you.

BEWARE THE ICE AT REIGATE
Belchwood Churchyard

JOHN ROSE
Died Jan. 27, 1810
Aged 10 years
Dear Friends and companions all,
Pray warning take by me,
Don't venture on the ice to far
As 'twas the death of me.

A FOOLISH MAN FROM WOODTON, NORFOLK

Here lies John Rackett
In his wooden Jacket;
He kept neither horses nor mules.
He lived like a hog,
And died like a dog,
And left all his money to fools.

ON MRS DEATH, THE WIFE OF A COMEDIAN

Here lies Death's wife. When this way next you tread,
Be not surprised should Death himself be dead.

THE UNMUSICAL MUSIC-MAKER
Youlgrave Churchyard

To the down Bow of death
His Forte gave way,
All the Graces in sorrow were drown'd;
Hallelujah Crescendo
Shall be his glad lay
When Da Capo the Trumpet shall sound.

To which someone added: 'The only connection he ever had with music was a mania for getting wood to make fiddle backs. He did not know the difference between G and A, nor even the half-tones in the octave.'

TO THE MEMORY OF A NABOB

Among the tombs in Westminster Abbey, is one to the memory of a Nabob, who is said to have acquired a large fortune in the East by dishonourable means. His ambition and his money ensured him a tomb in this the most famous cathedral in the world. The monument hints at his resurrection. The earth and sky is pictured on the slab as falling to pieces, while an angel sounds the last trump. The Nabob is shown as rising from the grave with a look of astonishment on his face, and opening a curtain to see what is the matter. The cruel cut of the epitaph is:

Lie still, if you're wise, you'll be damn'd if you rise.

THE INTERIOR WORKINGS OF LADY DODDERIDGE
Ob. 1614, Exeter

As when a curious clock is out of frame,
A workman all in pieces takes the same,
And mending what amiss is to be found,
The same rejoyns, & makes it true and sound;
So God this lady into two parts took,
Too soon her soul her mortal course forsook:
But, by His might, at length her body sound,
Shall rise, rejoyn'd unto her soul, encrown'd.
'Till then, they rest, in earth & heaven sunder'd,
At which conjoyn'd, all such as knew them wonder'd.

THE BAKER FROM RUIDOSO, NEW MEXICO

Here lies John Yeast
Pardon me for not rising.

A VILLAINS' DEED AT WORKINGTON
1808

You villains! If this stone you see,
Remember that you murdered me!
You bruised my head, and pierced my heart,
Also my bowels did suffer part.

N.B. Joseph Glendowing was murdered June 15, 1808, near Workington, Cumberland; the murderers were never found.

CAUSTIC COMMENT FROM WESTMINSTER ABBEY

Beneath this stone there lies a skull
Which, when it breathed, was wondrous dull.
But now 'tis dead, and doomed to rot,
This skull's as wise (pray is it not?)
As Shakespeare's, Newton's, Prior's or Gray's,
The wits, the sages of their days.

AN ORGANIST FROM WAKEFIELD, YORKSHIRE

In memory of
HENRY CLEMETSHAW
upwards of fifty years organist
of this church (Wakefield parish church), who died
May 7, 1821, aged 86 years.

Now like an organ, robb'd of pipes and breath,
Its keys and stops are useless made by death.
Tho' mute re-built by more than mortal aid,
This instrument, new voiced, and tuned, shall raise,
To God, its builder, hymns of endless praise.

LACKINGTON THE ECCENTRIC BOOKSELLER

Good passenger, one moment stay,
And contemplate this heap of clay;
'Tis LACKINGTON that claims a pause,
Who strove with death, but lost his cause.
A stranger genius ne'er need be
Than many a merry year was he.
Some faults he had, some virtues too
(The devil himself should have his due);
And as dame fortune's wheel turn'd round,
Whether at top or bottom found,
He never once forgot his station,
Nor e'er disown'd a poor relation;
In poverty, he found content
Riches ne'er made him insolent.
When poor, he'd rather read than eat,
When rich, books form'd his highest treat,
His first great wish to act, with care,
The sev'ral parts assigned him here;
And, as his heart to truth inclin'd,
He studied hard the truth to find.
Much pride he had —— 'twas love of fame,
And slighted gold, to get a name;
But fame herself prov'd greatest gain,

For riches followed in her train.
Much had he read, and much had thought,
And yet, you see he's come to naught;
Or 'out of print', as he would say,
To be revised some future day:
Free from errata, with addition,
A new and a complete edition.

ST EVERILDA'S CHURCH, EVERINGHAM
In memory of Jane Ward, died 1789

Here lies a maid to every good inclined,
Love by her neighbours, to her parents kind.
Trusting for bliss, in Christ she's gone before,
Changing her British for Emanuel's shore.
Being too good to live with earthly vice,
She's gone to feast in blooming Paradise.

THE SALISBURY CRICKETER

I bowl'd, I struck, I caught, I stopp'd,
Sure life's a game of cricket;
I block'd with care, with caution popp'd,
Yet Death has hit my wicket.

AT THE TOP OF A STAINED GLASS WINDOW IN A SUSSEX CHURCH

To the glory of God
and below
And in memory of his Grandfather

THE BRICKMAKER OF AWLISCOMBE, DEVON

Here lie the remains of
JAS. PADY, brickmaker
late of this parish
in hopes that his *clay* will be *remoulded* in a workmanlike manner far superior to his former perishable materials.

Keep death and judgement always in your eye
Or else the devil off with you will fly.
And in his *kiln* with brimstone ever fry.
If you neglect the narrow *road* to seek
You'll be rejected like a *half-burnt brick*.

FROM WORCESTER CHURCHYARD

Mammy and I together lived
Just two years and a half;
She went first —— I followed next,
The cow before the calf.

ROBERT CRYTOFT'S SOLILOQUY

Hamersfield Churchyard, Suffolk 1810

As I walk'd by myself, I talk'd to myself.
And thus myself said to me:
Look to thyself, and take care of thyself,
For nobody cares for thee.

So I turn'd to myself, and I answered myself,
In the self-same reverie:
Look to myself, or look not to myself,
The self-same thing will it be.

THE WORTH OF LORD POWIS'S DAUGHTER

O cruel cruel Death,
Thou hast taken away Lord Powis's eldest daughter's breath,
And here she lies under this here cold cold ground.
I daresay his Lordship would rather have given £100.

A NEW ENGLAND MAID

Beneath this silent tomb is laid
A noisy antiquated maid,
Who from her cradle talked till death
And ne'er before was out of breath.

IN THE CHURCH OF ST MARTIN, LEICESTER

Here lieth the body of
JOHN HEYWICK
of this parish, who departed this life
the second of April 1589
being about the age of seventy-six years.
He did marry Mary, the daughter of John Bond, of Warden, in
the county of Warwick, Esq.
He lived with the said Mary in one house full fifty two years,
and in all that time never buried
man, woman, nor child, though they were sometimes
twenty in household.
He had issue by the said Mary five sons and
seven daughters.
The said John was Mayor of the town
1559, and again in 1572.
The said Mary lived to ninety-seven
years and departed the 8th of
December 1611.
She did see, before her departure, of her children, and children's
children, and their children, to the number of 142.

AUGUSTA, MAINE, USA

Our little Jacob
Has been taken from this earthly garden
To bloom in a superior flower-pot
Above.

FROM DOUBLE BED TO DOUBLE GRAVE

To these, whom death again did wed
This grave's the second marriage bed;
For though the hand of fate could force
'Twixt soul and body a divorce,
It would not sever man and wife,
Because they both lived but one life.
Peace, good reader, do not weep;
Peace, the lovers are asleep;
They, sweet turtles! folded lie
In the last knot that love could tie;
Let them sleep, let them sleep on,
Till this stormy night be gone
And the eternal morrow dawn;
Then the curtains will be drawn,
And they wake into a light
Whose day shall never die in night.

UNLAMENTED FROM HENDON, MIDDLESEX

Beneath this stone Tom Crossfield lies,
Who cares not now who laughs or cries.
He laughed when sober, and when mellow.
He was a harum-scarum fellow
He gave to none designed offence,
So — *Honi soit qui mal y pense.*

The French tag — Evil be to him who evil thinks — is, of course, the motto of the British order of Chivalry, 'The Most Noble Order of the Garter' instituted in 1348.

JOHN CHEST OF CHEPSTOW

On the tombstone of the Rev. John Chest

Here lies at rest, I do protest,
One Chest within another.
The chest of wood was very good:
Who says so of the other?

UNLUCKY WILLIAM BECK

Here lies the body of WILLIAM BECK,
He was thrown at a hunt and broke his neck.

THE SWEET SMELLING PRIEST
Winchester College epitaph 1541

Beneath this stone lies shut up in the dark,
A fellow and a priest, yclep'd JOHN CLARK:
With earthly rose-water he did delight ye,
But now he deals in heavenly *aqua vitae*.

A SULLEN STORY

Here lies JOHN SULLEN, and it is God's will
He that was SULLEN should be sullen still;
He still is sullen, if the truth ye seek;
Knock until Doomesday, SULLEN will not speak.

IN A DEVONSHIRE CHURCHYARD

Charity, wife of Gideon Bligh,
Underneath this stone doth lie.
Nought was she e'er known to do
That her hisband told her to.

A SIGH OF RELIEF FROM CANTERBURY

Of children in all she bore twenty-four:
Thank the Lord there will be no more.

ON A YOUTH WHOSE NAME WAS CALF
Gloucester Cathedral

O cruel Death, more subtle than the fox,
To kill the Calf e'er he became an Ox.

CRUSTY MR BALL
From a Wiltshire Tombstone

Here I lie — my name is BALL —
I lived — I died, despised by all:
And now I cannot chew my crust,
I'm gone back to my ancient dust.

FOR A BAD VIOLINIST

When Orpheus played he moved Old Nick
But when you played you made us sick.

WORLDLY ADVICE FROM A LONDON CHURCHYARD

Stop, reader! I have left a world
In which there was a world to do;
Fretting and stewing to be rich —
Just such a fool as you.

THE SAILOR'S BRIDE
St Nicholas Church, Yarmouth

Here lies one, a sailor's bride,
Who widowed was because of the tide;
It drowned her husband — so she died.

THE SEX-STARVED BACHELOR
Braunston Churchyard, Northamptonshire

Tis true I led a single life,
And n'ere was married in my life;
For of that sex I n'ere had none;
It is the Lord: His will be done.

AN OLD FRENCH RHYME FROM CANTERBURY CATHEDRAL

Ou tu passe, j'ay passe;
Et par ou j'ay passe, tu passeras.
Au monde comme toi j'ai este
Et mort comme moi tu seras.

(Where now thou passest I have often passed
And where I have once, thou must also pass.
Now thou art in the world, and so was I;
And yet, as I have done, so thou must die.)

UNREQUITED LOVE FROM BIDEFORD, DEVON

The wedding day appointed was,
And wedding clothes provided;
But ere the day did come, alas!
He sickenéd and dieded.

SCOTTISH WISDOM

Here lies the body of GEORDIE DENHAM
If ye saw him now ye wadna ken him.

LETITIA THE FARMER'S DAUGHTER

Grim death, to please his liquorish palate
Has taken my LETTICE to put in his sallat.

POOR LITTLE ANGELINE!

Now Angeline was a harlot bold
Who's sleeping here in the frost and cold.
Stop, passer by! If you are willing
She was never known to refuse a shilling.

THE VALIANT CAPTAIN TULLY

Exeter Cathedral

Here lies the Body of Captain Tully,
Aged an hundred and nine years fully;
And threescore years before, as Mayor,
The sword of this city he did bear;
Nine of his wives do with him lie,
So shall the tenth when she doth die.

ROGER'S RAZOR SLIPPED

Here lies, alas! poor Roger Norton,
Whose sudden death was oddly brought on!
Trying one day his corns to mow off,
The razor slipped and cut his toe off!
The toe, or rather what it grew to;
The part then took to mortifying.
Which was the cause of Roger's dying.

A BYSTANDER'S COMMENT

From Painswick Church, Stroud, Gloucester

Take heed all ye who pass me by.
As you are now, so once was I.
As I am now, so you will be,
So be prepared to follow me.

To which some passer-by had added:
To follow you I'm not content
How do I know which way you went?

AN ODDITY IN GREENMOUNT CEMETERY, BALTIMORE

In a centrally located lot are three simple stones, on the first, in addition to the usual inscription for a deceased wife, has been chiselled an index hand. The hand points diagonally downwards towards the base of the central stone which indicates;

Hier ruht mein Mann (Here rests my husband)

The third stone, to the memory of a second wife, differs from the first in the mere matter of detail; a similar hand points downward:

Mien ist er auch (He is mine too)

As a climax of absurdity, however, crossed hands point serenely on a middle stone to the outlying mounds:

Diese beiden sind mein (These two are mine)

A husband thus erected three stones (one for himself to be used when the time came for his decease) in memory of his wives.

Franklin and Jefferson Wrote Their Own

As the tomb inscriptions of Ancient Egypt show, man has been writing epitaphs to praise, criticise, analyze and honour himself for more than five thousand years. In some cases, however, the composition of personal epitaphs was considered as necessary a task as writing a will, at least, both Benjamin Franklin (1706-90) and Thomas Jefferson (1743-1826) thought so.

Probably the first epitaph that Benjamin Franklin composed was that of his mother and father, Josiah Franklin and his (second) wife Abiah Folger. Under the heading 'Twyford, at the Bishop of St Asaph's 1771' (where he was holidaying with his dear friend Johnathan Shipley) in his 'Autobiography'

Franklin admits to writing this epitaph to his parents who 'died, he at eighty-nine and she at eighty-five years of age. They lie buried together at Boston where I some years since placed a marble stone over their grave with this inscription:

Josiah Franklin
And Abiah his wife
Lie here interred.
They lived lovingly together in wedlock
Fifty-five years.
Without an estate or any gainful employment,
By constant labour and industry,
With God's blessing,
They maintained a large family
Comfortably;
And brought up thirteen children,
And seven grandchildren
Reputably.
From this instance, Reader,
Be encouraged to diligence in thy calling,
And distrust not Providence.
He was a pious and prudent man,
She a discreet and virtuous woman.
Their youngest son,
In filial regard to their memory,
Places this stone
J. F. born 1655 – Died 1744 – AEtat.89.
A. F. born 1667 – Died 1752 – —— 85.

By my rambling digressions I perceive myself to be growing old. I used to write more methodically ...'

When writing his own epitaph (which was found among his papers after his death) revealed his own love of books ('From my infancy I was passionately fond of reading, and all the little money that came into my hands was laid out in the purchasing of books'):

The Body of
B. FRANKLIN
Printer
Like the cover of an old book,
its contents torn out,
and stripped of its lettering and gilding,
lies here, food for worms.
But the work shall not be wholly lost;
for it will, as he believed, appear once more,
in a new and more perfect edition,
corrected and amended
by the Author.
He was born January 6, 1706.
Died ——— 17—.

Thomas Jefferson, too, said 'I cannot live without books' and accumulated during his lifetime three major libraries (the first was burned at Shadwell, Virginia, his birthplace; the second was sold to the US Nation after the British fired the Capitol in 1814—this collection became the nucleus of the new Library of Congress; the third, some 1500 volumes, was scattered at the auction which followed his death) but there is no mention of this love in the record of how he wanted his epitaph set out.

In his own papers the self-taught architect wrote:

> Could the dead feel any interest in monuments or other remembrances of them, when as Anacreon says,
> 'A scanty dust to feed the wind,
> Is all the trace 'twill leave behind.'
> the following would be too my manes the most gratifying on the grave a plain die or cube of three feet without any mouldings, surmounted by an obelisk of six feet height, each of a single stone; on the faces of the obelisk the following inscription, and not a word more:

HERE WAS BURIED
T——— J———
AUTHOR OF THE DECLARATION OF AMERICAN INDEPENDENCE
OF THE STATUTE OF VIRGINIA FOR RELIGIOUS FREEDOM
AND FATHER OF THE UNIVERSITY OF VIRGINIA:

(N.B.—he omitted the fact that he had twice been
President of the USA)
because by these, as testimonials I have lived,
I wish most to be remembered. (It) to be of the
coarse stone of which my columns are made, that no
one might be tempted hereafter to destroy it
for the value of the materials. My bust, by
Ceracchi, with the pedestal and truncated column
on which it stands, might be given to the
University, if they would place it in the dome of
the Rotunda.
On the die of the obelisk, might be engraved
Born Apr. 2, 1743. O.S.
Died ———————

Jefferson's epitaph is to be seen at the family cemetery (still maintained as private property by Jefferson's descendants) not far from his former hilltop home of Monticello in Virginia's Albemarle County.

Others favoured lines more terse for their own epitaphs like Samuel Taylor Coleridge with:

Stop, Christian passer-by! — Stop, child of God.

While Fulke Greville's (First Baron Brooke 1554-1628) epitaph on his monument at Warwick reads more like a court circular:

Fulke Greville, Servant of Queen Elizabeth
Councillor to King James, and
Friend to Sir Philip Sidney.

Johnathan Swift (1667-1745), however, preferred his epitaph to be in the grand classical manner:

Ubi saeva indignatio ulterius cor lacerare nequit
Where fierce indignation can no longer tear the heart

Two British lawyers had a slightly different attitude to epitaph writing. Lord Brougham (1778-1868), one of the chief legal luminaries of the nineteenth century (who had made a great name by defending Queen Caroline against King George IV) wished to be remembered for his erudite spoken words:

> Here reader, turn your weeping eyes,
> My fate a useful moral teaches;
> The hole in which my body lies
> Would not contain one half my speeches.

while Lord Norbury wanted to be a learned wit to the end:

> He's dead! alas, facetious *punster*,
> Whose jokes made learned wigs with fun stir;
> From heaven's high court, a tipstaff[1] sent,
> To call him to his *pun*-ishment:-
> Stand to your ropes! ye sextons, ring!
> Let all your clappers, ding, dong, ding!
> Nor-bury him without his due,
> He was himself a Toler[2] too.

Count Tessin, a governor of King Gustavus III of Sweden, required only two words on his monument:

TANDEM FELIX (Happy at last!)

For a long time Hollywood has been the centre of America's glittering society life and hostesses there have spared no expense to entertain their guests.

During the 1930s one bright, twittering society dame thought up the idea of amusing her guests by commissioning a witty author to compose humorous epitaphs for them. The hostess, who had been an actress herself and much married, set the ball rolling by having her epitaph written. As it was read out by the author at one of her famous parties, however, the hostess's face was seen to change colour for he had written:

At last she sleeps alone!

[1] A constable
[2] A family of noted lawyers

Many famous people have written their own epitaphs prematurely, of which the following are but a brief example:

Hendrick Willem Van Loon, (1882-1944), Dutch-American historian:

Here lies
HENDRICK WILLEM VAN LOON
Oh wanderer, if my wish could come true
Then you would be I, and I would be you.

Thought to have been written by one of the famous Marx Brothers (Groucho, Harpo, Chico, Zeppo):

Here lie the
FOUR MARX BROTHERS
The first time they ever
went out together.

George Gershwin, (1898-1937), American jazz pianist and song writer:

Here lies the body of
GEORGE GERSHWIN
American Composer.
Composer?
American?

Michael Arlen, (1895-1956), naturalised British novelist:

Here lies
MICHAEL ARLEN
As usual.

Marc Connelly, (b.1890) American Dramatist:

Here lies Marc Connelly
Who?

Sherwood Anderson (1876-1941), American author:

Good night,
'Twas Fun Enough, and life was dear,
I tried to get my wish,
I did not want to die —
Before they put me here.

George Arliss, (1868-1946), stage and film actor:

All my old junk gone to the storehouse,
Here I am God, starting for your house.
In order to prevent possibility of ruction,
Am bringing you back your original production.

Rex Ellingwood Beach, (1877-1949), American novelist:

Here lies
REX BEACH
Teed up 1867. Bunkered 19—
He worked a little, and played
enough at the fairway, but fetched
the rough.

Sir Jacob Epstein, KBE, (1880-1959), New York born sculptor:

From life's grim nightmare he is now released
Who saw in every face the lurking beast.
'A loss to All', says friends both proud and loyal,
'A loss' say others, 'to the Café Royal'.

Gustave Flaubert (1821-80), French novelist:

Un fois je pense: 'Il faut que je vive.'
Mais maintenant, je dit: 'Je n'en vois pas la nécessité.'

Earl David Lloyd George of Dwyfor, (1863-1945), British Prime Minister:

Count not my broken pledges as a crime,
I MEANT them, HOW, I meant them at the time.

Tombstone Epilaughs

AN INTERNATIONAL COLLECTION OF EPITAPHS

Wyoming County, New York

> She was in health at 11.30 a.m.
> And left for Heaven at 3.30 p.m.

Ithaca, New York

> While on this earth my knee was lame,
> I had to nurse and heed it
> But now I've gone to a better place,
> Where I don't even need it.

Of a Paris Brothel-owner

He gladdened many hearts.

The Miller from Toulouse

Alas friend Pierre
His end was very sudden
As though a mandate came
Express from Heaven.
His foot did slip, and he did fall.
Help, help, he cried, and that was all.

Beware skating at Nantes

Dear friends and companions all
Pray warning take from me.
Don't venture on the ice to far
For 'twas the death of me.

The tomb of an English mercenary at Lille

Oh, Cruel Death, to make three meals in one,
To taste and taste till all was gone.
But know, thou Tyrant, when the trump shall call
He'll find his feet and stand when thou shall fall.

(Apparently this soldier first lost a toe through gangrene, afterwards a leg, and then his life).

A glutton of Nice

This disease you'll never discover
I died from eating melon.
Be careful then all those who feed
For I was ere a glutton.

Two Unfortunate British trainspotters!

Llanmynech Graveyard, Wales

In crossing o'er the fatal bridge
John Morgan he was slain.
But it was not by mortal hand,
But by a Railway train.

Martham Cemetery, Norfolk

Though shot and shell around flew fast
On Balaclava's plain,
Unscathed he passed to fall at last,
Run over by a train.

The Engineer from St Lawrence, Hungerford, Berks

Passengers of every age
I safely drove from stage to stage,
Till Death came by in a hearse unseen,
And stopped the course of my machine.

The Decimal children!

	Born	Married	Died	Issue
Here lyes Robert Short	1612		1699	6.2
Wright in Ross		1664		
and Janet Kirkpatrick	1644		1735	
his spouse.				
James Short Marchant	1677	1723	1752	2.4
in Mossall.				
Alexr. Henry and	1670	1712	1745	
Margrat Thomson his				
spouse.	1674		1746	2.1
Also Elizabeth Graham	1720	1747	1756	1.2
spouse to Mr Thomas				
Henry, Surgeon, also	1710		1803	
the said Thomas Henry				
Surgeon, also	1733		1808	2.1
Isabella Graham his				
second spouse.				

Garrel Churchyard, Kirkmichael, Dumfriesshire

Unlucky Mr Lamb from Huntingdon

On the 29th November
A confounded piece of timber
Came down, bang slam
And killed I, John Lamb.

The Halmstad gossip, Sweden

Short and happy was my life,
But sudden was my death.
One moment talking to my friends
The next, I lost my breath.

Lines on a stubborn husband from Dun Dealgan, Eire

Here lies the body of Robert Moore.
What signifies more words?
He killed himself by eating curds.
But if he'd been ruled by Sarah, his wife,
He might have lived out all the days of his life.

Brotherly love from Ulster

Erected to the memory of
John Phillips
Accidentally shot
As a mark of affection by his brother.

Castle Caldwell, Lough Erne, Eire

To a drunken fiddler who drowned in the Lough—the memorial tablet is in the shape of a violin:

August ye 15
1770
Beware ye fidlers of ye fidlers fate
Nor tempt ye deep least ye repeant to late
Ye ever have been deemed to water foes
Then shun ye lake till it with whiskey floes
On firm land only exercise your skill
There you may play and drink your fill.

Groningen, Holland

From the grave of a senior citizen:

Do not mock an old woman.
No one knows his fate
From old age and death God alone is free
All other things change with time
And that means you.

The Downs from South Australia

In memory of
Eileen, Ida, Ben and Bob
DOWN

A triad from Whitby, Yorkshire

The illness laid not in one spot,
But through his frame it spread.
The fatal disease was in his heart,
And water in his head.

Sudden and unexpected was the end
Of our esteemed and beloved friend.
He gave to all his friends a sudden shock
By one day falling into Sunderland Dock.

To Rose Herring

The freshest of all Herrings once was this,
Sweet as the new-born Rose.
In hope of awakening to eternal bliss,
Now in foul pickle she doth here repose.

Soporific Isle of Wight!

Here lies the body
Of Samuel Young
Who came here and died
For the benefit of his health

From a Churchyard near North Down, Northern Ireland:

RIP until the next General Election.

From a Somerset Churchyard

Here lies the body of JAMES ROBINSON and RUTH his wife
'Their warfare is accomplished.'

Shropshire Verbosity

ELIZABETH,
the wife of Richard Barklamb,
passed to eternity on Sunday, 21st May, 1797,
in the 71st year of her age.
RICHARD BARKLAMB
the ante-spouse uxorious,
was interred here 27th January, 1806,
in his 84th year.
WILLIAM BARKLAMB
brother to the preceding, Sept. 5th, 1779,
aged 68 years.

When terrestriall all in chaos shall exhibit
effervescence,
Then celestial virtues, in their most refulgent brilliant
essence,
Shall, with beaming beauteous radiance, thro' the
ebullition shine,
Transcending to glorious regions beautiful sublime.
Human power, absorb'd deficient to delineate such
effulgent lasting sparks,
When honest plebians ever, will her presidence o'er
ambiguous great monarchs.

Greedy Tam Reid

Here lies TAM REID
Who was chokit to deid
Wi' taking a feed
O'butter and breed
Wi' owre muckle speed,
When he had nae need,
But just for greed.

English versions of some German epitaphs

Of a bachelor

At threescore winters' end I died,
A cheerless being, sole and sad,
The nuptial knot I never tied, —
And wish my father never had.

To all my friends I bid adieu.
A more sudden death you never knew.
As I was leading the old mare to drink
She kicked and killed me in a wink.

Oh Lord, here I lie, and no wonder I'm dead
A thumping great waggon went over my head.

Heinrich Muller's best bedroom.

Hackney Churchyard, London

As still as death poor Peter lies,
And Stiller when alive was he,
Still not without a hope to rise
Though Stiller then he still will be.

(From the tomb of one Peter Stiller).

Yarmouth Cemetery

Owen Moore has gone away,
Owin' more than he can pay.

Lee County, Mississippi

Once I Wasn't.
Then I Was.
Now I ain't again.

Richard Button from Salisbury

Oh Sun! Moon, Stars and Celestial Poles!
Are graves then dwindled into Buttonholes?

Walton Graveyard, Norfolk

Here lies Matthew Mudd, death did him no hurt.
When alive he was but Mudd, and now dead, he's but dirt.

Llangerrig Cemetery, Montgomeryshire, Wales

From earth my body first arose,
But here again to earth it goes.
I never desire to have it more
To plague me as it did before.

Lancello, Cornwall

You was left to me when you was young.
Your mother eloped, and she was wrong.

Warrington Cemetery, Lancashire

This maid no elegance of form possessed,
No earthly love defiled her breast.
Hence free she lived from the deceiver—man,
Heaven meant it as a blessing—she was plain.

From a graveyard in the Isle of Wight

Here lies Margaret, otherwise Meg,
Who died without issue, save on her leg.
Strange woman, she, and extremely cunning,
For whilst one leg stood still, the other kept running.

An Uncle from Cheshire

Beneath this stone, a lump of clay,
Lies Uncle Percy Daniels.
Too early in the month of May
He cast his winter flannels.

John Blackburn's come-uppance, from Scothorne Graveyard, Lincolnshire

Alas poor John
Is dead and gone,
Who often tolled the bell,
And with a spade
Dug many a grave
And said Amen as well.

Ockham Church, To the Memory of One John Dyer

A Dyer by name, and a dyer by trade,
Of a dire disease he a dier has made;
But mark you, that it may seem very quaint,
A dier he was of a liver complaint.

From Great Walford Churchyard, Worcestershire

John Randall, 1699

Here old John Randall lies,
Who counting from his tale
Lived three score years and ten,
Such virtue was in Ale.
Ale was his drink
Ale was his meat
Ale did his heart revive,
And if he could have drunk his Ale
He still had been alive.
But he died January five
1699

Epitaph in an Essex country churchyard

Underneath this tuft doth lie
Back to back my wife and I.
Generous stranger, spare the tear,
For could she speak, I cannot hear.
Happier far than when in life,

Free from noise and free from strife.
When the last trump the air doth fill,
If she gets up then I'll lie still.

Mr Knott from Perth

Here lies a man who was Knott born;
His father was Knott before him.
He lived Knott, and he did Knott die,
Yet underneath this stone doth lie.
Knott christened,
Knott begot.
And here lies,
And yet was Knott.

A Bath Abbey memorial

These walls adorned with monumental busts
Show how Bath waters serve to lay the dust.

Sarah Ricketts, died 1767, of Barking, Essex

Here honest Sarah Ricketts lies,
By many much esteemed,
Who really was not otherwise
Than what she ever seemed.

A message from Mr Pocock, North Curry, Somerset

My good lads, do not sit upon this stone
On account you do disfigure it with your heels;
Lean on it if you please.
Yours &,
R. Pocock.

The miser's tomb, Dorchester Abbey, Oxford

Here lieth one who for medicine would not give
A little gold: and so his life was lost.
I fancy that he'd wish again to live
Did he know how much his funeral cost.

All is not what it appears at Hornsey Churchyard, London

To the memory of Emma and Maria Littleboy, the twin children of George and Emma Littleboy of Hornsey, who died July 16th, 1837

TWO LITTLEBOYS LIE HERE, YET STRANGE TO SAY
THESE LITTLEBOYS ARE GIRLS

Of Mr Peck from Oxford

Here lies a Peck, which some may say
Was first of all a Peck of clay.
This wrought with skill divine while fresh,
Became a curious Peck of flesh.
Through various forms its Maker ran,
Then adding breath, made Peck a man.
Full fifty years Peck felt life's troubles
Till Death relieved a Peck of troubles;
Then fell poor Peck, as all things must,
And here he lies — a Peck of dust.

From Narrow-on-Soar, Leicestershire

Here in this grave there lies a Cave.
We call a cave a grave.
If cave be grave, and grave be cave,
Then reader, judge, I crave,
Whether doth Cave lie here in grave
Or grave here lie in cave:
If grave in cave here buried lie,
Then grave, where is thy victory?
Go, reader, and report here lies a Cave
Who conquers Death, and buries his own grave.

In Memoriam Mr Cave

Of Anne Roberts, an actress, who died in 1743

The World's a Stage, at Birth our Play's begun,
And all find Exits when their Parts are done.

And, of John Smith the Oyster-seller of Childwall, Lancashire

Here lies the body of John Smith, Buried in the cloisters.
If he don't jump at the last trump, Call 'Oysters'.

Although plain postcards were offered for sale at British Post Offices from 1 October 1870 (a year after their introduction in Austria-Hungary), it was not until around 1894 that the first British commercially produced picture postcards appeared. Among the early picture postcard designs were such tombstone memorials as the Wordsworth Grave (Grasmere, Westmorland) and the John Ruskin Memorial (Coniston, Lancashire), and which were very popular from the late 1890s; later there were to appear on postcards the more lengthy epitaphs like the now world famous 'Unknown Warrior's Grave in Westminster Abbey, London:

GREATER LOVE HATH NO MAN THAN THIS
IN CHRIST SHALL ALL BE MADE ALIVE
UNKNOWN AND YET WELL KNOWN
DYING AND BEHOLD WE LIVE
THE LORD KNOWETH THEM THAT ARE HIS

BENEATH THIS STONE RESTS THE BODY
OF A BRITISH WARRIOR
UNKNOWN BY NAME OR RANK
BROUGHT FROM FRANCE TO LIE AMONG
THE MOST ILLUSTRIOUS OF THE LAND
AND BURIED HERE ON ARMISTICE DAY
11 NOV : 1920. IN THE PRESENCE OF
HIS MAJESTY KING GEORGE V
HIS MINISTERS OF STATE
THE CHIEFS OF HIS FORCES
AND A VAST CONCOURSE OF THE NATION

THUS ARE COMMEMORATED THE MANY
MULTITUDES WHO DURING THE GREAT
WAR OF 1914-1918 GAVE THE MOST THAT
MAN CAN GIVE LIFE ITSELF
FOR GOD
FOR KING AND COUNTRY

FOR LOVED ONES HOME AND EMPIRE
FOR THE SACRED CAUSE OF JUSTICE AND
THE FREEDOM OF THE WORLD
THEY BURIED HIM AMONG THE KINGS BECAUSE HE
HAD DONE GOOD TOWARD GOD AND TOWARD
HIS HOUSE

Later the Ministry of Works were to produce a lengthy series of postcard views which incorporated gravestone pictures like the interesting collection from Lindisfarne Priory, from Holy Island off the coast of Northumberland, England.

The other protagonists of the picture postcard, France and Germany, produced various graveyard views like *Le Tombeau de Napoleon 1er—Chapelle des Invalides, Paris* (Napoleon 1's tomb—Chapel of the 'Hospital for Disabled Soldiers', Paris) and *Tombeau de Richard Coeur-de-lion* at Rouen Cathedral and the heavy Teutonic graveyard masonry, including, rather oddly, selections of 'foreign cemeteries' (i.e., Parnell's Grave, Glasnevin, Dublin) of the German postcard manufacturers.

Strangely enough these gravestone picture postcards sold in large quantities and were sent by holidaymakers back home with as much regularity as the 'pretty pretty scenes' and the comic postcard. Unfortunately some of the senders did not realize the unconscious humour they were instigating in their messages.

On the back of postcards in the author's collection are these cryptic comments:

View	*Message*
St Tudno's Cemetery, Llandudno the tomb of *Ivy Grace Brown*	Sent: 6 July, 1911 'Dear Dollie — I shall not be able to come this week as Ma has made other arrangements for tomorrow — Yours *Florence Grace Brown*'
Margate, Kent Surf Boat Memorial	Sent: 13 August 1913 'We have arrived safely—Love Lily'
St Martin's Graveyard Canterbury	Sent: 5 June 1900 'Dear Mother-in-law—Wish you were here—George'

North Country Epitaphs

Holy Trinity, Skipton

Here lies Bob Saunders, who received a thump
Right on the forehead, from the village pump.
He saw bright stars until the end
And many doctors did his case attend.

St John the Baptist, Knaresborough

Here lies, praise God, a woman who
Scolded and stormed her whole life through:
Tread gently o'er her rotting form
Or else you'll raise another storm.

St Mary the Virgin, Richmond

Beware proud stranger who'ere ye be
For thou might'st end up like me.
Grim death took me without any warning
I was well at night, but died in the morning.

All Saints, Kirbymoorside

Death will'd that Robert WILLING here should lie
Although unwilling he to die.

St Mary-le-Gill, Barnoldswick

Here lies one Thomas Foote
Whose bones may hundreds save
For death now has one foot
Entombed within the grave.

St Mary, Bridlington Priory

Suddenly and unexpected was the end
Of our respected friend.
To all his friends a sudden shock he gave
By one day falling from this towering nave.

St Peter, Conisborough

A heavy stone on me did fall
And killed me dead against yon wall.
Yet epitaphs are all but stuff
Here lies a sinner: That's enough.

St Oswald, Filey

Here lies the body of Billie Round
Lost at sea and never found.

All Saints, Hooton Pagnell

Our zealous sneak-thief dy'd of late
And did arrive at Heaven's gate.
He stood without and would not knock
For he preferred to pick the lock.

St Mary's, Hull

Around here lies the bones of Stephen Nokes
Who lived and loved, and died like other folks.
For nigh on thirty years he told the bell
To tell the villagers around that all was well.
Stephen and Time are now both even
Stephen kept Time—now Time keeps Stephen.

All Saint's, Northallerton

Here lies my wife in earthly mould,
Who, when alive did naught but scold.
Pray, wake her not, for now she's still
At last indeed, I have my will.

Parish Church, Richmond

Here lies entombed beneath this flag, the corpse of
WILLIAM WIX
He lived and died like other folks, was always full
of tricks:
One thousand seven hundred and sixty-six.

St Mary, Beverley

Beneath this stone our Grandam Lays
She used to ride and shoot with hounds
She lived 80 years and 20 days
And cost us many pounds.

From the tomb of William Harrison, Hessel Road Cemetery, Hull

Long time I ploughed the ocean wide,
A life of toil I spent;
But now in harbour safe arrived
From care and discontent.

My anchor's cast, my sails are furled
And now I am at rest;
Of all the ports throughout the world,
Sailors, this is the best.

Kirk Hammerton Churchyard

Here lies the swift racer, so famed for his running
In spite of his boasting, his swiftness and cunning;
In leaping o'er ditches, and skipping o'er fields
Death soon overtook him, and tript up his heels.

Winstone Churchyard

Where I am gone, you are coming;
So be serious, stop your funning.

Selby Abbey

(Eye) Findeth : (Heart) Choseth : (Knot) Bindeth
(Death) Looseth

Darlington Church

Here lye the bodies of CHARLOTTE SCOULAR, buryed by this stone who dyed on January 13th 1731: Likewyse here lyse dear JOHNATHAN SCOULAR, hyr husbande and ryte hand, who was buryed on that same day come seven years, 1738.

In seven years' time there comes a change,
Observe, and here you'll see,
On that same day come seven years
My husband's laid by me.

West Boldon Church

This tomb, which once bore an iron pan has now been removed; the pan was fixed onto the original gravestone by the wish of the deceased.

WILLIAM CHALKELEY—IRONMONGER—AET 1798

Here lies my corpse, who was the man, that loved a sop in the dripping pan.
But now, believe me, I am dead, see how the pan stands at my head.
Still for the sops till the last I cried but could not eat, and so I died.
My neighbours, they perhaps will laugh, when they do read my epitaph.

Easington Church.

Such is our lot—We linger out the day;
Who stays the longest has the most to pay.

St Hilda's, Hartlepool

Ephraim Judd: The Card Maker

His card is cut: Long days he shuffled through
The game of life: He dealt as others do.
Though he by honours tells not its amount
When the last trump is play'd, his tricks will count.

Gateshead Churchyard; In memory of the Architect of the Exchange and Guildhall

Here lies ROBERT TROLLOPE
Who made your stones roll up.
When Death took his soul up
His body fill'd this hole up.

Monkwearmouth, Anglo Saxon Church

Dear Mates and Cronies all,
Pray warning take by me:
Don't venture in the sea too far,
For't was the death o'me.

Escomb Church

Weep not for me, my husband dear,
Keep it in mind that I lies here.
And when thou'st scour'd and cleaned and pined
Think on, why I left it all behind.

* * *

Here lieth Andrew Broadhead
Who died from cold caught in the head

It brought an ague and rheumatiz
Which ended me—for here I is.

Youth was his age
Virginity his state
Learning his love
Consumption his fate.

Fragment from the Chapel, Durham Castle

It seems as if nature had curiously plann'd
That men's names with their trade should agree.
There's Thweeping, the teaman, who's laid near at hand
Would be weeping, if robbed of his T.

From a stone discovered at the church of St Mary-le-Bow, North Bailey, Durham City, during the restoration of 1875: The stone was resealed in the west wall:

As careful nurses to their bed doe lay,
Their children which too long would wanton play;
So to prevent all my ensuing crimes,
Nature, my nurse, laid me to bed betimes.

In Horsley Church, Cumberland

Here lie the bodies
Of THOMAS BOND and MARY his Wife.
She was temperate, chaste, and charitable;
But, she was proud, peevish, and passionate.
She was an affectionate wife, and a tender mother;
But, her husband and child, whom she loved,
seldom saw her countenance without a disgusting frown,
whilst she received visitors, whom she despised, with
an endearing smile.
Her behaviour was discreet towards strangers;
But, imprudent in her family.
Abroad, her conduct was influenced by good breeding;
But, at home, by ill temper.
She was a professed enemy to flattery,

and was seldom known to praise or commend;
But, the talents in which she principally excelled
were difference of opinion and discovering
flaws and imperfections.
She was an admirable economist, and, without prodigality
dispensed plenty to every person in her family;
But would sacrifice their eyes to a farthing candle.
She sometimes made her husband happy with her good qualities;
But, much more frequently miserable with her many failings;
Insomuch, that in thirty years' cohabitation
he often lamented
that, maugre all her virtues
he had not, in the whole, enjoyed two
years of matrimonial comfort.
At length, finding she had lost the affection of her
husband, as well as the regard of her neighbours,
family disputes having been divulged by servants,
she died of vexation July 20, 1768 aged 48 years.
Her worn out husband survived her four months and
two days, and departed this life Nov 28th 1768.

William Bond, brother of the deceased, erected this stone as a weekly monitor to the surviving wives of this parish that they may avoid the infancy of having their memories handed down to posterity with a patch-work character.

Parish Church, Carlisle

Reader, of these four lines take heed,
And mend your life for my sake
For you must die, like Archie Reed,
Tho' you read till your eyes ache!

A Carlisle Innkeeper

Hark! Hark ye, old friend! what will pass then without
Taking notice of honest plump Jack?
You see how't is with me, my light is burnt out,
And they've laid me here flat on my back.

The woolcomber from Workington, who was hanged for sheepstealing

Here lies the body of Arnold Kemp,
Who lived by wool, but died by hemp;
There's nothing would suffice this glutton,
But, with the fleece, to steal the mutton.
Had he but work'd and lived uprighter,
He'd ne'er been hung for a sheep-biter.

Charlotte Palmer of Penrith

By his kind help, who sits on Heaven's throne,
I reached the reverenced age of ninety-one,
At eighty-seven I had a broken shin,
At eighty-nine I halved my dose of gin.

And being come to ripe maturity
Plac'd all my thought upon futurity,
Thinking I heard a bless'd angel say
Cheery old soul! pack up and come away!

The Blacksmith from Brampton

My sledge and hammer lie reclined,
My bellows too have lost their wind.
My fire's extinct, my Forge decayed,
And in the dust my vice is laid;
My coals are spent, my iron's gone,
May nails are drawn, my work is done.

Maryport's Celestial Traveller

Ann Brown left Maryport and started for Paradise 25 June 1801

Keswick Knowledge

Make me to mind Eternal things
That when I come to die
My soul may clap her joyful wings,
And climb her native sky.

From graveyards around Whitehaven

You who are in health as once was I
Freed from great trouble in the dust to lie.
Remember this, that you must die.
May Church and state ever defended be
From Popish plots, pride and conspiracy. 1774

On Joan Bates and her daughter
We two within this grave do lye,
Where we do rest together;
Until the Lord shall us awake,
And from the goats us sever.

Here lies at rest in sweet repose,
Cropt by death's hand, a budding rose:
Beloved by all, her parents pride,
Who never grieved them till she died.
Emily Rice, 1886

Reader reflect, repent, believe, amend
Time has no length, Eternity no end.

On a sea captain and his wife
Here we lie in a horizontal position, like a
Ship laid up, stripped of her sails and rigging.

Unveil, thy bosom faithful tomb,
Take this new treasure to thy trust,
And give these sacred relics room,
Awhile to slumber in the dust.

Reflections from Westmorland

I coo and pine and ne'er shall be at rest
Till I come to thee, dearest, sweetest, best.

Thomas Walker,	died	Agnes Walker
aged 56	1865	aged 91

Short and uncertain is the life of man,
His life's a vapour, and his time's a span,
His days alas! are swifter than a post,
He passes by, and in the grave is lost.

William Jones
Florist of Appleby
died 1833, aged 67 years

Yes, he is gone, and we are going all,
Like flowers we wither, and like leaves we fall;
He worked like Adam among the shrubs and trees,
And view'd his labour 'midst the humming bees.

Eliza, sorrowing, rears this marble slab
To her dear Peter, died from eating crab.

Here lies John and Sarah and Mary too,
They were quins, see what God can do,
First died ye daughters, then ye sonne,
Three days between. Thy will be done.

Epitaph for a dog buried outside Windermere Cemetery

Thou who passest on the path, if haply thou dost mark this monument, laugh not, I pray thee, though it is a dog's grave; tears fell for me, and the dust was heaped above me by a master's hands, who likewise engraved these words on my tomb.

Sacred to the memory of the Reverend Ralph Tyrer, Vicar of Kendal, who died AD 1627

London bred me—Westminster fed me,
Cambridge sped me—My sister wed me,
Study taught me—Living sought me,
Learning brought me—Kendal caught me,
Labour press'd me—Sickness distress'd me,
Death oppress'd me—The grave possess'd me,
God first gave me—Christ did save me,
Earth did crave me—And Heaven would have me.

On Robert Lambe, 1799

O Lambe of God, which sin did take away,
And as a Lambe was offered up for sin,
When I, poor Lambe, went from thy flock astray
Yet thou, good Lord, vouchsafe thy Lambe to win
Home to thy fold, and hold thy Lambe therein,
That at the day when lambes and goates shall sever
Of thy choice, Lambe may be one for ever.

Here lies a woman
No man can deny it,

She died in peace, although she lived in quiet;
Her husband prays, if e'er this way you walk,
You would tread softly—if she' wake she'll talk.
Troutbeck, Westmorland.

This poem was written by Alexander Pope for one John Knight who lies buried in Gosfield Churchyard, Essex. The epitaph was utilised by another of the same name at Appleby.

O fairest pattern to a falling age,
Whose public virtue knew no party rage,
Whose private name all titles recommend,
The pious son, fond husband, faithful friend;
In manners plain, in sense alone refined,
Good without show, and without weakness kind;
To reason's equal dictates ever true,
Calm to resolve and constant to pursue;
In life, with every social gift adorned,
In death, by friendship, honour, virtue, mourned.

Another from Troutbeck

If Bowness village you should know,
There may you hear my fyles to go,
Pins and needles, sirs, who buyes 'em,
Hard and sharp, whoever tryes 'em,

Toys and rattles to still babyes,
Temple wires, that's fit for laydes.
Come and buy, if you'll have any,
I wod fain draw the packing penny.
Whilst the pedlar thus doth bawle,
And his wares for sale doth call,
Death passes by like one unknown,
Commands him pack—His market's done.

On John Hill of Manchester

Here lies JOHN HILL
A man of skill
His age was five times ten;
He ne'er did good,
Nor ever would,
Had he lived as long again.

Hale Churchyard, Lancashire

Borne 1598 Dyed 1623
Here lyeth the bodie of John Middleton
The Childe, nine feet three.
On the 'Childe of Hale'.

Stand Church, near Manchester

See Father, see the Mother cries,
This child has got a fit;
But now beneath this stone it lies
This world it soon did quit.

St John's Church, Burnley; from the tomb of William Pepper

Tho' hot my name, yet mild my nature,
I bore good will to every creature;
I brewed good ale and sold it too,
And unto each I gave his due.

St Elphin's Church, Warrington

This stone is not to be disturbed after the interment
of
JOHN LEIGH

The old Quay Flats was my delight;
I sail'd in them both day and night.
God bless the Masters and the Clerks,
The Packet people and Flatmen too,
Horse drivers and all their crew.
Our sails are set to Liverpool,
We must get under way—
Discharge our cargo safe and sound
In Manchester Bay.
Now all hands when you go home
Neither fret any nor mourn;
Serve the Lord where'er you go
Let the winds blow high or low.

Mary Leigh, his sister, died October 6th, 1801, aged 26 years;
Betty, mother of John and Mary Leigh, died 6th May 1826,
aged 88 years

To our God let us pray
Keep us from drunkenness and wickedness both night and day
This stone and grave is free gift of John Yates, Mariner
Captain of the Old Quay Packet.
God bless all English Sailors Admiral Nelson, and all the fleet
When we must go, we do not know, sweet Jesus Christ to meet.

St Ann's Churchyard, Manchester

Here lie interred the remains (which through mortality are at present corrupt, but which shall one day surely be raised again to immortality and put on incorruption) of Thomas Deacon, the greatest of sinners and the most unworthy of primitive Bishops, who died 16th of February 1753 in the 56th year of his age; and of Sarah, his wife, who died July 4th 1745, in the 45th year of her age. The Lord grant unto the faithful here underlying that they may find mercy from above for all the wrongs they did in life which vexed their parishioners.

Newton Heath, near Manchester

The following is copied from a slab bearing masonic markings

I H S

The remains of CHARLES ASHWORTH of Manchester here doath lie

His better Parts are in the Lodge on High
The Level's worth he knew upright and fair
And as a Brother departed on the Square
Yon Glorious Arch to Contemplation upon
That Valiant mystery of the three in one.

Ralph and John Wood, Undertakers, Salford

We that have made tombs for others,
Now here we lie:
Once we were two flourishing Woods—
But now we die.

On a Wealthy Oldham Merchant, Josiah Perkins

A man of wealth and fame
Of honour and of worth;
How powerful was his name
When living on the earth.
But now he's left the world
Where riches draw a line
Distinguishing a man
From others of his kine.
What now can this man do
With what he had whilst here?
Not aught, for what he had—
In heaven it can't appear.
We speak of him 'in heaven',
Well, let us hope he's there;
Though the chances of such men
To get there are but rare.

From a Wesleyan Chapel, Bolton

Her manners mild, her temper such
Her language good, and not too much.

Thomas All, the Rochdale weaver

Reader, beneath this marble lies
ALL, that was noble, good and wise;
ALL, that once was formed on earth,
ALL, that was of mortal birth;
ALL, that liv'd above the ground,
May within this grave be found:
If you have lost or great or small,
Come here and weep, for here lies ALL;
Then smile at death, enjoy your mirth,
Since God has took his ALL from earth.

AUTHOR'S NOTE

While all the foregoing epitaphs are authentic and genuine, in that they once embellished the tombs of the deceased, it should be noted that as time passes they become less and less accessible.

Church renovation, weather, vandalism and many other reasons may have caused some of the epitaphs to be moved from their original sitings, thus the collector should not be surprised nor disappointed if they are not to be found where quoted in the text.

Index